The Changing Role of the Human Resource Profession in the Asia Pacific Region

T0348776

ELSEVIER
ASIAN STUDIES SERIES

Series Editor: Professor Chris Rowley,
Centre for Research on Asian Management,
Cass Business School,
City University, UK; HEAD Foundation, Singapore
(email: c.rowley@city.ac.uk)

Elsevier is pleased to publish this major Series of books entitled Asian Studies: Contemporary Issues and Trends. The Series Editor is Professor Chris Rowley, Director, Centre for Research on Asian Management, City University, UK and Director, Research and Publications, HEAD Foundation, Singapore.

Asia has clearly undergone some major transformations in recent years and books in the Series examine this transformation from a number of perspectives: economic, management, social, political and cultural. We seek authors from a broad range of areas and disciplinary interests covering, for example, business/management, political science, social science, history, sociology, gender studies, ethnography, economics and international relations, etc.

Importantly, the Series examines both current developments and possible future trends. The Series is aimed at an international market of academics and professionals working in the area. The books have been specially commissioned from leading authors. The objective is to provide the reader with an authoritative view of current thinking.

New authors: we would be delighted to hear from you if you have an idea for a book. We are interested in both shorter, practically orientated publications (45,000þ words) and longer, theoretical monographs (75,000−100,000 words). Our books can be single, joint or multi-author volumes. If you have an idea for a book, please contact the publishers or Professor Chris Rowley, the Series Editor.

Dr Glyn Jones
Email: g.jones.2@elsevier.com

Professor Chris Rowley
Cass Business School, City University
Email: c.rowley@city.ac.uk
www.cass.city.ac.uk/faculty/c.rowley

Elsevier Asian Studies Series

The Changing Role of the Human Resource Profession in the Asia Pacific Region

Jayantee Mukherjee Saha

Chris Rowley

ELSEVIER

AMSTERDAM • BOSTON • HEIDELBERG • LONDON • NEW YORK • OXFORD
PARIS • SAN DIEGO • SAN FRANCISCO • SINGAPORE • SYDNEY • TOKYO

Elsevier
Radarweg 29, PO Box 211, 1000 AE Amsterdam, Netherlands
The Boulevard, Langford Lane, Kidlington, Oxford OX5 1GB, UK
225 Wyman Street, Waltham, MA 02451, USA

ISBN: 978-0-85709-475-9

British Library Cataloguing-in-Publication Data
A catalogue record for this book is available from the British Library

Library of Congress Cataloging-in-Publication Data
A catalog record for this book is available from the Library of Congress

Library of Congress Control Number: 2014952990

For Information on all Elsevier Publishing publications
visit our website at http://store.elsevier.com/

Typeset by MPS Limited, Chennai, India
www.adi-mps.com

Contents

Foreword by Dave Ulrich

I can still recall in another time and place starting my PhD research on the Japanese and US electronics industries. At the time, the emerging electronics industry and Japanese management were two of the 'hottest' business topics. Decades later, the industries have dramatically evolved, as has the focus on Japanese management. Japanese management practices (e.g., lean manufacturing) are still relevant, but there has been a dramatic shift from just focusing on Japan to all of Asia.

No one doubts that Asia is going to be the economic powerhouse for the next decade at least. Moreover, people are beginning to realize that Asia is not a single set of ideas embedded across countries, but consists of unique actions in rapidly growing economies from China to India to Indonesia to Malaysia to Vietnam to Philippines to Sri Lanka to (fill in country).

In these vibrant and growing economies, consumers are expecting and receiving products and services. Organizations in these economies are continuing to innovate not only in their manufacturing operations, but also their organization capabilities. Many Asian organizations have created strong organization capabilities through their talent, leadership, and culture. Human resource professionals have become the architects of these organization capabilities. They ensure that talent, leadership, and culture reflect changing consumer expectations and business conditions.

As HR professionals throughout Asia strive to build the right organization, they ensure financial success through quality disciplines, firm/government collaboration, customer connections, organization accountability, talent development, and leadership excellence.

In this exceptional volume, we receive deep insights into six industries across Asia: tourism/hospitality, retail, healthcare, education, security, and energy. By sharing insights across these industries and across countries, the authors show that Asian human resources can continue to provide insights that can be transferred to the rest of the world.

Little did I realize decades ago that Japanese management would morph into Asian human resources, and the electronics industry would evolve to include nearly all industry segments. What a marvelous time to learn from great practices in so many industries and so many countries.

Dave Ulrich
Rensis Likert Professor, Ross School of Business,
University of Michigan, Alpine, Utah, USA

Foreword by Peter Cappelli

Asia, especially Southeast Asia, is experiencing an unprecedented period of economic growth, in which business is generating opportunities and demands faster than most societies can keep up with. Nowhere is this more apparent than in employment. Rural workers with little or no experience of regular employment are being pulled from farms into factories, newly minted managers with little or no experience are being put in charge of them, and employers find themselves crafting policies and practices as they go.

Although they have often mastered and even innovated in areas like logistics and production systems, these new companies find topics like recruiting, selection, and particularly retention little more than mysteries. Practices that tie employees to the employer and prevent the revolving door that otherwise occurs are still to be developed. Most importantly, policies that have transformed the lives of workers elsewhere and their societies, such as insurance plans, retirement programs, and anti-discrimination practices, are still waiting to be discovered.

The story in this volume deals with the way in which good employment principles that have been developed elsewhere can transform both Asia's burgeoning businesses as well as the communities in which they operate. It is a story that deserves to be taken seriously, not just by employers but by policy makers in Asia and in the international agencies that advise them.

Peter Cappelli
George W. Taylor Professor of Management and Director,
Center for Human Resources, Wharton School of the
University of Pennsylvania, Philadelphia, PA, USA

Foreword by Prabir Jha

"Everyone, from the doorman to the Chairman, has a view about HR. None is wrong, even though none may be right. This is the nature of the beast that is called HR, or the people agenda. As the world changes, business models evolve and talent gets re-defined, the centrality of HR as a business success determinant becomes more pronounced. It is in this context that Jayantee Mukherjee Saha and Chris Rowley have produced a very insightful book, based on their research of six focus industries across seventeen countries in the Asia Pacific region, a clutch of economies that form more than one-third of the world GDP at purchasing power parity and is home to half the world's population – the largest potential consumer base.

The book has presented a wonderful collection of lucid stories that show the opportunity and challenges that industries in the region are confronted with. It also is an equally smart introspection on how the HR function increasingly can impact labour market efficiency. In a market where talent is getting sharply re-defined and the societal values still hold a deep imprint on labour market nuances, the examples shared remind us of how the new must juxtapose itself with the old, not blindly repudiate it. It is a sharp reminder to all policy shapers that the future growth of this region will rest on how well various industries are served by an altered reality of contemporary labour markets, often with sub-regional angularities. It thus presents a very comprehensive ring side view of the intersect of economics, business, labour markets and HR leadership in the region, something that gets any reader of economics and HR absorbed and reflective. The book will attract the interest of business leaders, policy formulators, HR thinkers and HR students.

The problems and opportunities shared in the various case studies could trigger profound discussions among HR practitioners, both learnings and newer postulates. A neat compilation like this is not an answer to all HR problems but is more a platform that encourages collective learning by academics and practitioners alike. Every case has reflections and similarities with pour own experiences, making the book immensely readable and valuable.

Most important of all, the book crystal gazes into the world of tomorrow through the changing profiles of HR leaders in the region. The book has a particularly refreshing section, aptly captioned, "Like it or Loathe it", based on analysing the social media profiles of senior HR professionals in the region. As the region increases opportunities based on technology and social media becomes a key enabler of brands, the changing social media profiles of HR leaders shows how talent magnets of tomorrow will be created. The war for talent will no doubt be the war of brand recall of companies, its business leaders and, not surprisingly, its HR leaders.

I am sure that "The Changing Role of the Human Resources in the Asia Pacific Region" will cause enlightenment and excitement in a diverse stakeholder community in a region that will attract substantial global interest in the days ahead. As HR professionals grapple with the business possibilities and talent challenges in the region, this book will help prepare minds of those who seek to win this war for talent and, thus, business. Agility, comfort with ambiguity, creativity, customer-centricity and most of all combining the mind with the heart is what it will take to be a victor in the business battlefields of the Asia Pacific. For soldiers and generals alike, Jayantee has produced a master piece. One can ignore the wisdom only at one's own peril".

Mr. Prabir Jha

President & Group CHRO, Reliance Industries Limited (RIL) Mumbai, India.

Acknowledgements

We extend our gratitude to Dave Ulrich (Rensis Likert Professor, Ross School of Business, University of Michigan), Peter Cappelli (George W. Taylor Professor of Management and Director, Center for Human Resources, The Wharton School, University of Pennsylvania) and Prabir Jha (President and Group CHRO, Reliance Industries Limited) for their encouraging and insightful forewords.

We also want to thank Dee Pak Behl (Director, HR, The Grand, New Delhi), Dilep Misra (President, Corporate HR, JK Organization), Eddie Lee Senior (HR professional at a major international airways company operating in Singapore), Madhu Dubey (Regional Director, India Tourism, Sydney), Manoj Kumar Sharma (Senior Vice President, HR, AMR, India), Martin Duffy (General Manager, Human Resources, OfficeWorks), Rajeev Kumar (General Manager, Learning and Development, Tata Group Corporate Communication), Udayan Dutt (Director, HR, Unilever, Sri Lanka) and Wayan Carma (Director, HR and Finance, Singgasana Hotels and Resorts, Indonesia) for supporting the study and sharing their experiences with us.

Finally, we thank Glyn Jones and his colleagues from the publishing team for all their efforts in working with us on this book.

About the author

Jayantee Mukherjee Saha is Director and Principal Consultant of Aei4eiA Pty Ltd. Aei4eiA is a Sydney-based management/policy research and consultancy firm focusing on 'People and Sustainability' matters. She has extensive experience in the fields of business strategies, management/policy research, people management & organisational development. She has held senior positions with professional bodies and academic institutions and works closely with Government/public sector agencies, MNCs/SMEs, global bodies and academic institutions spread across the Asia Pacific and the UK.

Jayantee regularly contributes to forums, been invited columnist in leading HR/business magazines in the APAC region and has over 50 publications, including three books, to her credit. She has received many awards and her work has been widely acclaimed by practitioners and scholars alike.

She takes active interest in Social Justice Causes (that include employment and labour market, multicultural diversity and inclusiveness) and believes Social Justice and sustainability are interlinked. Currently, she is the Deputy Chairperson of Access & Social Justice Consultative Group at one of the Local Government Councils (in Sydney) with responsibilities to advocate for an accessible and socially just inclusive community. She is also a planning committee member of a Multicultural Network facilitated by the local Government which aims to identify and address issues affecting people from Culturally And Linguistically Diverse (CALD) backgrounds in area. She holds- PhD (Management); MPhil. (Management); MBA (Human Resources Management); BSc. (Physics, Chemistry and Mathematics); Certificate in Human Rights; Certificate in 'Towards an inclusive society: how to tackle discrimination in the world of work', conducted by the International Labour Organisation (ILO).

Professor Chris Rowley is Director of Research and Publications, HEAD Foundation, Singapore and Professor of Human Resource Management at Cass Business School, City University, London, UK. He is Editor of the leading journal Asia Pacific Business Review, Series Editor of the Working in Asia and Asian Studies book series. He has given a range of talks and lectures to universities and companies internationally with research and consultancy experience with unions, business and government. Professor Rowley has published widely in the area of HRM and Asian business, with over 500 articles, books and chapters and practitioner pieces.

Introduction

1

Introduction

The human resource (HR) profession has been on a long and challenging journey. Globalisation and sweeping policy changes are factors that have redefined and realigned HR and its role in the organisation. The HR function may be seen as having evolved not only over time, but content. There are many typologies and frameworks showing this such as those proposed by Tyson and Fell (1986). Others like Ulrich (1997), Ulrich, Younger, Brockbank, and Ulrich (2012) and Welch and Welch (2012) present different types of framework. What these convey is that the title of HR manager covers a wide range in terms of the content of the job, with greater or fewer levels on reactive – proactive or operational – strategic spectrums (Rowley & Jackson, 2011).

While explaining the business partner model, Ulrich and Brockbank (2008) pointed out that HR plays a significant role in the creation and maintenance of capabilities an organisation must have in order to deliver value to its customers, shareholders, employees and communities. Generally speaking, HR has evolved from just being transactional to being a strategic business partner, from being a cost centre to profit centre partnering business growth (Moore & Furlong, 2012). The post-2008 global financial crisis made it clear that economies were not just facing another cyclical economic downturn but in its wake came impactful, structural, demographic and mindset changes across various industries. Business leaders could not afford to respond with anything less than a major overhaul of the HR management (HRM) system to survive and sustain – HR as a practice and profession needs to 'transmute' (Mukherjee Saha, 2010, p. 21).

Our book addresses a set of interrelated questions. What are the principal challenges HR is facing? Given each industry has its own complexities, is it not a necessity to assess and analyse industry-specific HR challenges and best practices? Can HR take on the responsibility of increasing productivity in industries? With the rapid changes going on in workplaces and economies, is it not a prerequisite for HR professionals to develop competencies and enhance knowledge and by so doing have an effect on their respective industries (Ulrich et al., 2012)?

The premise of our book rests on the principle of laws of attraction, which claims that 'thoughts become things'. In this world of business uncertainties and corporate fragilities, acknowledging good HR policies and practices can certainly influence the economic, societal and environmental aspects of an organisation. It may further trigger collective thinking on the part of the HR and business community, economies and societies at large for transmutation to take place for the common good (Mukherjee Saha, 2010, p. 21).

The book covers the following six key industries: (1) tourism and hospitality, (2) retail, (3) healthcare, (4) education, (5) security; (6) energy (including oil, gas and renewables). There is copious evidence that these industries play major roles in economies (as explained in Chapter 2). A closer look reveals the interdependence of these, something that will be elaborated in the following chapters. Industry-level analysis backed up by case studies of organisations from specific industries and operating in the region has been included to further elaborate the concept.

Why focus on the region?

The greater Asia Pacific (GAPAC) is that part of the world in or near the western Pacific Ocean. We take its main economies to include Australia, Cambodia, China, Hong Kong, India, Indonesia, Japan, South Korea, Malaysia, Myanmar, New Zealand, the Philippines, Singapore, Sri Lanka, Taiwan, Thailand and Vietnam. The GAPAC region/zone is also a term often used by UN agencies (UN-ESCAP, 2010).

With each passing year, the region is becoming ever more significant for both positive and negative reasons. Home to about half the world's population, diverse groups of people, huge repositories of natural resources and some of the world's largest militaries, the region is the key engine driving the global economy (VOA, 2012). With a huge consumer base and attracting investors from all over the world, the region accounts for over one third (almost 37 per cent) of world gross domestic product (GDP) at purchasing power parity (PPP).[1] The region is dynamic and is expected to become the growth centre of the world by 2025 (APFED, 2005). Table 1.1 indicates the importance of the region by providing some HR and economic statistics.

Over the years, the region has become ever more resilient at withstanding global financial shake-ups and the consequent economic slowdowns (Mukherjee Saha & Ang, 2014). There are two reasons for such resilience: first, the demand for exports of goods and services from advanced economies and, second, increasing domestic demand. Growth in Asia is highly export dependent and heavily tilted towards the tradeable sector — where output is determined in terms of goods or services traded domestically or internationally. Manufacturing, consulting, energy, engineering and finance are examples of tradeable sectors. As a result of globalisation, Internetisation, information flows across country borders and, consequently, more informed consumer bases, the expectation of quality products and services both for export and internal consumption is on the increase. Such demands for quality products and services will require increases in productivity and reforms in product, HR and financial markets, as well as in fiscal and exchange rate policies (IMF, 2010). To cope with the increase in demand for quality products and services and maintain productivity levels, such a shift requires HR reskilling. Thus, knowledge, which is fundamental to the service sector, will become increasingly important as a source of productivity growth and improvement in organisational capabilities.

Table 1.1 A few vital statistics on people and economy in the GAPAC region

Economies	Population (million, as of July 2013, rounded up)	Population rank in the world (as of July 2013)	Median age of population (as of July 2013, rounded up)	Population below poverty line (% as of July 2011, rounded up)	Literacy rate (% of total population)	Total labour force (million; as of July 2013, rounded up)	Percentage of labour force by sector (2011 estimate, rounded up)			GDP at purchasing power parity (in US$ billion, estimated 2012)	Stock of foreign direct investment at home (in US$ billion as of December 2012)	Stock of foreign direct investment at home (rank in the world as of December 2012)
							Agriculture	Industry	Services			
Australia	22	57	38	NA	99	12.15	4	21	75	961	610.8	13
Cambodia	15	69	24	20	74	7.9	56	17	27	36.5	NA	NA
China	1349	1	36	13	95	798	35	29	36	12,260	1344	3
Hong Kong	7	100	44	NA	94	3.79	0	6.70	93	365.6	1422	2
India	1220	2	27	30	63	482	53	19	28	4710	225.1	23
Indonesia	251	5	29	12	93	118	35	20	45	1200	192.7	27
Japan	127	11	46	16	99	65	4	26	70	4570	222.2	25
South Korea	48	26	40	17	98	25.5	6	24	70	1590	147.2	30
Malaysia	29	44	27	4	93	12.9	11	36	53	494.7	132.4	35
Myanmar (Burma)	55	25	28	33	93	33.4	70	7	23	102.6	NA	NA
New Zealand	4	125	37	NA	99	2.38	7	19	74	131	81.36	43
Philippines	105	13	23	26	95	40.4	32	15	53	419.6	30.38	61
Singapore	5	115	34	NA	96	3.36	0.10	20	80	323	741	10
Sri Lanka	21	59	31	8	91	8.46	32	26	42	125	NA	NA
Taiwan	23	52	39	1.50	96	11.34	5	36	59	894	59.36	51
Thailand	67	21	35	8	94	39.4	38	14	48	645	185.7	28
Vietnam	92	15	29	11	95	52	48	21	31%	336	73.71	48

Source: CIA, 2014.

Historically, the region's economic development has largely been driven by adopting a labour-intensive, export-oriented development strategy of key industries, supported by heavy exploitation of HR and natural resources (APFED, 2005, p. 14). GAPAC used to be dominated by agriculture, but it is gradually shifting its focus to the industry and services sectors. Only four economies in the region still have most of their labour force working in the agriculture sector, whereas for thirteen the majority are working in the services sector (Table 1.1).

Paradoxically, along with the economic potential and the availability of human and natural resources, the region has to grapple with fierce social challenges like poverty, nutrition and health, education, discrimination and corruption. Research highlights the need for the region to undergo structural transformation (ADB, 2013). Such challenges put pressure on the environment, and its degradation poses a serious threat to the region's growth prospects. Moreover, the region is disaster prone suffering frequent natural disasters like earthquakes and tsunamis (Table 1.2). The region is also the epicentre of many conflicts, political instability and pandemics (UN, 2013).

Therefore, the region's efforts to sustain economic prosperity, withstand the challenges mentioned above and improve productivity receive a lot of attention. Indeed, the region is home to major industries and companies and has been attracting many investors from around the world. Twelve of the region's economies in 2012 were ranked among the top-50 preferred economies for foreign

Table 1.2 Disaster statistics from 1980 to 2010

Country	Natural disasters from 1980 to 2010 (number of events)	Average number of people killed per year	Economic damage per year (US$ × 1000)
Australia	162	31	926,451
Cambodia	31	63	17,294
China	597	5018	11,059,134
Hong Kong	58	17	17,498
India	431	4614	1,550,446
Indonesia	321	6209	761,344
Japan	157	276	6,717,123
South Korea	71	105	479,662
Malaysia	58	40	60,242
Myanmar	27	4491	149,859
New Zealand	44	1	151,961
Philippines	363	1063	239,263
Singapore	3	1	0
Sri Lanka	62	1193	54,012
Taiwan	65	131	623,596
Thailand	105	385	194,282
Vietnam	159	519	256,637

Source: PreventionWeb, 2013.

direct investment (FDI). FDI stock gives the cumulative US dollar value of all investments in the home country made directly by residents – primarily companies – of other countries. It excludes investment made by the purchase of shares (Table 1.2).

Taking all of this on board, it makes sense to take a closer look at the dynamics these industries generate and how they affect sustainable development of the region overall while maintaining its position as a global growth engine. As the region continues to be labour intensive, we focus on the role, efficiency, effectiveness, issues and challenges facing HR productivity and the role the HR profession and professionals play in this context. As a result of limited resources, we focus on six key industries: (1) tourism and hospitality, (2) retail, (3) healthcare, (4) education, (5) security, (6) energy (including oil, gas and renewables).

Focus industries and changing role of HR

The rationale behind our choice of focus industries relates to their increasing significance in the region's economies and emerging challenges. A closer look reveals the interdependence of these industries. We now turn to the key points that will be elaborated in the following chapters.

1. Tourism and hospitality

Tourism and hospitality represents the world's largest industry and the largest creator of jobs across national and regional economies. Jobs are spread across the economy – in retail, construction, manufacturing and telecommunications – as well as directly within the industry. Tourism can also be one of the most effective drivers for the development of economies, both developed and emerging (WTTC & IHRA, 1999). The ability of tourists to gain easy access to countries has resulted in increased global competition within the industry to attract tourists. There are many prerequisites to becoming a tourist destination, including how well a society treats its visitors. Does HR have a role to play in developing a communication channel and establishing a social dialogue? While tourism can bring positive benefits, there are perils like natural disasters, economic downturns, terrorism and health pandemics that need to be taken into account. How prepared is tourism's HR to deal with such challenges and sustain growth in the industry? What role can HR play to help minimize business risk?

2. Retail

Retail is in constant flux characterized by the wide variety of products offered, customer sophistication, use of technology for online purchases, price wars, etc. The region faces a complex range of challenges, from economic slowdowns, increases in consumer debt levels and dampening of retail property markets in some countries, like Australia, to upbeat consumers or optimistic customers in countries like India and China. To remain competitive, retailers must take a methodical and well-directed approach to understanding their business and delivering customer delight (i.e., the result of delivering a product or service that exceeds customer expectations; Braxton Group, 2012). Yet, what is the best way to delight customers? Has talented, customer-focused, engaged HR anything to do with it? Though the significance of engaged and customer-focused HR is well reinforced by many researchers, all customers can relate to the influence customer-facing employees have on them. Studies indicate that relatively low employee engagement levels have significant implications for Asian retailers. Can HR create a culture of employee engagement, thereby adding to the business bottom line?

3.   Healthcare

Healthcare plays a role in everyone's life, from pre-birth to post-death. It has an important contribution to make to economies and helps determine GDP. The human touch is key to every aspect of the industry. With increasing life expectancy, ageing populations and a plethora of health-related problems and ongoing medical advances, this industry will grow and grow. Yet, it has been facing challenges like acute HR shortages of carers and clinical staff and long waiting times for patients. The World Health Organisation (WHO) points out that developed countries experience HR shortages as a result of the growth of their ageing populations and increasingly high-tech healthcare. At the same time, government and universities have underinvested in health worker education, often leaving countries with insufficient new health workers to replace colleagues who retire. On the other hand, developing countries face HR shortages of their own, with overworked doctors struggling to fight epidemics, catching the illness and on occasion succumbing to it. Moreover, many healthcare workers migrate to wealthier nations and, as a consequence, HR shortages in poorer nations worsen (WHO, 2011). HR has a role to play in key areas like attracting and retaining talent, succession planning and dealing with regulatory matters.

4.   Security

Security is a basic human need, be it in the workplace, home or in public. As crimes become ever more complex, ranging from cyber to missile attacks, the significance of the security industry grows in importance. However, the industry is neither well defined nor clearly identifiable (ECORYS, 2009). The sensitive nature of this industry adds to the paradox of whether it should be clearly defined or left alone. The industry is of paramount importance to the continued success of any business or economy. All our other focal industries are very much interrelated with the security industry, which plays the unique role of helping sustain them all. The industry has progressed immensely, moving beyond looking after physical safety to issues such as the online security concerns of business, energy security, background checks, business risk management and audits. For instance, the safety and security sector has been identified as one of the five global forces driving tourism (Leong, 2000). In the energy industry, the focus of energy security has traditionally been on accidents and natural disasters. However, 9/11 changed all that with policymakers and industry experts starting to focus on the resilience of the energy system or energy security (Brown, Rewey, & Gagliano, 2003). Moreover, the United Nations identified global terrorism as one of the top-three socioeconomic issues (together with global warming and global ageing; UN, 2001) that need to be addressed. In the healthcare industry, the importance of adequate healthcare background screening became abundantly clear by the case of healthcare nurse Charles Cullen who confessed to murdering up to 40 patients in hospitals in Pennsylvania and New Jersey despite being fired at least five times by previous facilities (ARS, 2011). Do organisations have enough skilled HR to take care of these growing needs? Could HR help streamline industries by better defining the job scope of HR and training/retraining HR to keep up to date with the latest security requirements.

5. Education

More and more economies around the region are striving to be knowledge societies by both educating and skilling future and current HR. HR is expected to fill talent gaps in various industries and serve as one of the key ingredients to a competitive economy. However, issues concerning HR in the education sector have come under greater scrutiny. Studies have reinforced the fact that HRM in the sector is still relatively underdeveloped and has a long way to go. A key HR challenge currently being implemented concerns academics brought in to play the role of line managers. HR has a major role to play in monitoring the monitors.

6. Energy (including oil, gas and renewables)

Energy is central to social and economic development and is important in poverty alleviation. On the one hand, economic growth, rising standards of living and consumption patterns have increased the demand for energy, whereas much of the population in the region has no access to modern energy services (UN-ESCAP, 2001), on the other hand. The industry includes organisations dealing with its production and sale (both renewable and non-renewable). It is key to fuelling the growth and development of many other industries including tourism and retail. HR challenges are primarily in the areas of workplace safety (where lack of knowledge and mistakes can result in serious accidents causing irreparable damage), industrial relations, training, spreading awareness about environmental issues and encouraging innovation.

Research and methods

This book is based on research and industry-level analysis that have a geographical focus on the GAPAC region. The research was conducted by Aei4eiA (Australia) in 2012–13. The research steps taken were as follows.

Identification of geographical focus

The GAPAC region was chosen as the focus of this research; it is that part of the world in or near the western Pacific Ocean. It comprises such countries as Australia, Cambodia, China, Hong Kong, India, Indonesia, Japan, South Korea, Malaysia, Myanmar, New Zealand, the Philippines, Singapore, Taiwan, Thailand and Vietnam. GAPAC is a term often used by UN agencies (UN-ESCAP, 2010).

Focus industries

Six industries were chosen for the purpose of this research: retail, tourism, healthcare, security, education and energy. The rationale behind the choice was explained in the 'Why focus on the region?' section.

Industry-level analysis

The analysis includes industry overviews, factors that affect growth, government regulations, leading businesses, key industry-specific HR/business challenges, the preparedness of workforces to deal with such challenges and the role HR can play to minimize business risks, add to business bottom lines and sustain industry growth overall. A literature review was conducted. The search included research papers published in journals available in online databases (primarily EBSCO), Internet search engines (primarily Google and Yahoo), news scanning, industry reports and official statistics such as census figures. The key words used for the search related to HR practices in the six focus industries and the industries themselves.

Case study

Ten cases (Table 1.3) were developed using the random purposeful sampling method. This method can be used to sample a specific group of people within a population. Senior managers/business heads from organisations operating in the region and pertaining to the focus industries were chosen. From an internal database of Aei4eiA, some 40 organisations (limited due to resource constraints) belonging to the industry sectors in question and operating in the region were randomly picked and cases developed. Eight in-depth interviews (either via telephone or face-to-face of approximately 60 minutes each) were conducted and the remaining two were carried out via email. Though this method has its limitations in terms of generalising the overall population, it allows researchers to pull information-dense data points

Table 1.3 **Number of organisations by sectors ($n = 10$)**

Industry sector	Accepted (number)	Economy representing	Representatives from organisations
Education	01	India	Tata Group
Energy	02	India	JK Group, AMR
Healthcare	01	China	GlaxoSmithKline
Retail and consumer	02	Australia, Sri Lanka	OfficeWorks (Australia); Unilever (Sri Lanka)
Security	0	—	—
Tourism and hospitality	04	Australia, India, Indonesia, Singapore	India Tourism (Sydney); Grand Hotel (New Delhi); Singgasana Hotels & Resorts (Indonesia); a major international airways company (Singapore)

from the population, making it possible to come up with interesting inferences. Interviews are particularly useful at getting to the heart of the story and to the details and nuances behind a participant's experiences. This allows the interviewer to pursue in-depth information around the topic (McNamara, 1999). Interviews were complemented with secondary sources. This included the websites, annual reports and newsletters of organisations; news published in the media; and traditional sources like books and journals.

Structure of the book

This book is somewhat unusual in nature in that it not only assesses and acknowledges industry-specific HR challenges, but also suggests HR practices and processes that might help improve the industry in question. It highlights the role that the HR profession and its practitioners, policies and practices could play. The book presents an integrated approach where interlinkages between industries have been noted. Our book has a further five chapters. Chapter 2 provides an in-depth analysis of the six industries (tourism and hospitality, retail, healthcare, education, security and energy including oil, gas and renewables) across the GAPAC region. The business dynamism and complexity of each particular industry are detailed, as are the competitive advantages and their significance for the region's economies and the rest of the world. Chapter 3 analyses how HR as a profession has evolved within particular industries across the region and indicates gaps that need to be filled. Chapter 4 notes a few HR so-called 'best practices' (see Rowley & Wei, 2011 on limits to this) adopted by such organisations in specific industries in the region. Chapter 5 is based on the relatively new concept that HR can play a role in sustaining the business growth of industries across the region. Finally, Chapter 6 summarises the book and concludes that HR can be key to creating economic, environmental and social growth. The approach is based on the premise that organisational HR policies and practices can, once properly aligned, provide a direct and economically significant contribution to organisational performance.

Conclusion

Over the years the region has become the epicentre of global activity, both in terms of maintaining the region's economic prosperity or protecting the environment for the greater good of the world (Mukherjee Saha & Ang, 2014). Now, Western and more developed economies and companies look toward the region as a global growth engine that could be harnessed to leverage further development of their respective economies. This changing epicentre of global activity demands further analysis of such dynamism.

This chapter introduces the context of this book and sets the stage for Chapter 2, which introduces the theme of the book and looks at the changing role and significance of human resources, the HR profession and function, and their policies and practices in the GAPAC region.

Note

1. A nation's GDP at PPP exchange rates is the sum value of all goods and services produced in the country valued at prices prevailing in the US in the year noted (ECB, 2008).

References

ADB. (2013). *Asia's economic transformation: Where to, how, and how fast? Key indicators for Asia and the Pacific 2013*. Manila, the Philippines: Asian Development Bank.

APFED. (2005). Overview of the Asia-Pacific Region. *Asia-Pacific Forum for Environment and Development*. Available from: <http://www.apfed.net/pub/apfed1/final_report/pdf/overview.pdf> Accessed 14.10.13.

ARS. (2011). *Health care background screening is of critical importance*. Advanced Research Systems. Available from: <http://www.arsbackgrounds.com/health_care_background_screening.html> Accessed 30.05.12.

Braxton Group. (2012). Glossary. Available from: <http://www.braxton-network.com/resources/resources/best-practice/best-practice-resources/glossary/> Accessed 30.05.12.

Brown, H., Rewey, C., & Gagliano, T. (2003). *Energy security, national conference of state legislatures*. Washington, DC: The Forum of America's Ideas.

ECB. (2008). *Asia's economic transformation: Where to, how, and how fast?* European Central Bank. Available from: <http://www.ecb.europa.eu/press/key/date/2008/html/sp080225.en.html> Accessed 16.10.13.

ECORYS. (2009). *Study on the competitiveness of the EU security industry*. Brussels: Directorate-General Enterprise & Industry.

IMF. (2010). *Regional economic outlook: Asia and Pacific: Leading the global recovery: Rebalancing for the medium term.* Washington, DC: International Monetary Fund.

Leong, C. C. (2000). Strategies for safety and security in tourism: A conceptual framework for the Singapore hotel industry. *Journal of Tourism, 11*(20), 44–52.

McNamara, C. (1999). *General guidelines for conducting interviews.* Robbinsdale, MN: Authenticity Consulting.

Moore, K., & Furlong, R. (2012). The human resources department as a profitability factor. Available from: <http://humanresources.about.com/od/humanresourcesstrategic/a/hr_profit_2.htm> Accessed 30.05.12.

Mukherjee Saha, J. (2010). *HR transmutation: Path to progress.* Singapore: HumanCapital, pp. 21–23.

Mukherjee Saha, J., & Ang, D. (2014). *HR transmutation: The changing HR landscape across the Asia Pacific Region.* Sage. (Under publication).

Rowley, C., & Jackson, K. (Eds.). (2011). *Human resource management: The key concepts.* London: Routledge, pp. 7–10.

Rowley, C., & Wei, Q. (2011). Best practice. In C. Rowley, & K. Jackson (Eds.), *Human resource management: The key concepts* (pp. 7–10). London: Routledge.

Tyson, S., & Fell, A. (1986). *Evaluating the personnel function.* London: Hutchinson.

Ulrich, D. (1997). *Human resource champions: The next agenda for adding value and delivering results.* Cambridge, MA: Harvard Business School Press.

Ulrich, D., & Brockbank, W. (2008). The business partner model: 10 years on – lessons learned. *HR Magazine, UK.* Available from: <http://www.hrmagazine.co.uk/hr/features/1014777/the-business-partner-model-lessons-learned#sthash.tLehnyra.dpuf> Accessed 01.06.14.

Ulrich, D., Younger, J., Brockbank, W., & Ulrich, M (2012). *HR Talent and the New HR Competencies.* RBL. Available online at <http://rbl-net.s3.amazonaws.com/hrcs/2012/HRtalent-HRcompetencies.pdf> Accessed 23.02.14.

UN. (2001). *World population prospects: The 2000 revision.* New York: United Nations.

UN. (2013). *Enhancing knowledge and capacity to manage disaster risk for a resilient future in Asia and the Pacific.* New York: United Nations.

UN-ESCAP. (2001). *Bali declaration on Asia-Pacific perspectives on energy and sustainable development – sustainable energy development action programme, strategies and implementation modalities for the Asian and Pacific region, 2001–2005.* New York: United Nations.

UN-ESCAP. (2010). Asia-Pacific Trade Facilitation Forum 2010: Trade Facilitation for Regional Connectivity: Advancing Paperless Trade. Available from: <http://www.unescap.org/tid/projects/tfforum.asp> Accessed 30.05.12.

VOA. (2012). The importance of the Asia-Pacific region. *Voice of America.* Available from: <http://editorials.voa.gov/articleprintview/1514099.html> Accessed 16.10.13.

Welch, C., & Welch, D. (2012). What do HR managers do? HR roles on international projects. *Management International Review, 52*(4), 597–617.

WHO. (2011). Health Service Delivery. Available from: <http://www.who.int/healthsystems/topics/delivery/en/index.html > Accessed 10.06.13.

WTTC, & IHRA. (1999). *Tourism and sustainable development: The global importance of tourism, United Nation's Department of Economic and Social Affairs.* New York: World Travel and Tourism Organization and International Hotel and Restaurant Association.

Six major industries: An overview | 2

Introduction

In Chapter 1 we discussed the significance of the region. In this chapter we take a closer look at the six focus industries: tourism and hospitality, retail, healthcare, education, security and energy (including oil, gas and renewables). The 17 regional economies we consider are Australia, Cambodia, China, Hong Kong, India, Indonesia, Japan, South Korea, Malaysia, Myanmar (Burma), New Zealand, the Philippines, Singapore, Sri Lanka, Taiwan, Thailand and Vietnam. The business dynamism and complexity of each particular industry along with competitive advantages and their significance on the region's economies and the rest of the world (ROW) are reviewed in the following sections.

Tourism and hospitality industry

According to the United Nation's World Tourism Organization (WTO), 'Tourism comprises the activities of persons traveling to and staying in places outside their usual environment for not more than one consecutive year for leisure, business and other purposes' (WTO, 1993). Tourism is one of the most important industries in the world and is growing at a rapid pace. In 2012 the industry recorded one billion international tourist arrivals for the first time in history. WTO records indicate that tourism contributes 9 per cent to world GDP and US$1.3 trillion to exports. One in eleven jobs globally is in tourism. Interestingly, the region is one of the fastest growing in the world in terms of tourism, recording 16 million more tourists in 2012 (WTO, 2013). Tourism is a highly resource base-dependent industry and environmental quality is of utmost significance when tourists choose a destination. Fennell (1999) describes sustainable tourism development as needing to: (i) develop greater awareness and understanding of tourism's significant contributions to the environment and the economy; (ii) promote equity and development; (iii) improve host communities' quality of life; (iv) provide high-quality experience for visitors; (v) maintain environmental quality.

Apart from briefly describing country-specific issues and challenges, we provide four broad parameters of the total contribution made by the industry over time (2009–13): (a) employment, the number of jobs generated directly plus indirect and induced contributions; (b) GDP, that generated directly plus indirect and induced contributions including capital investment spending; (c) capital investment, spending by all sectors directly involved in the industry and investment spending by other industries on specific tourism assets such as visitor accommodation and leisure facilities; (d) domestic spending, as carried out within a country by its residents for both business and leisure trips.

Tourism and hospitality industry: Australia

In Australia, tourism ranks among the most significant industries and contributes heavily to the economy. Natural landscapes, the indigenous culture and heritage make Australia an interesting tourist destination. 'There's nothing like Australia' is Tourism Australia's (the Australian government agency responsible for promotion of the industry) global consumer marketing campaign. Recent records note that every dollar spent on tourism generates an additional 91 cents in other parts of the economy. In 2013 the industry contributed over US$150 billion to GDP. With almost 280,000 enterprises operating within the industry, it is a major creator of jobs (Table 2.1). Tourism is also the largest service export industry. However, high Australian dollar rates and competition from other global markets are two key challenges.

To cope with these challenges and sustain growth, Tourism Australia has recently devised a strategy called 'Tourism 2020'. It is a whole government approach to improving the industry's productive capacity and is devised to increase the return from the industry. It has identified six strategic areas that need to be focussed on: (i) growing demand from Asia; (ii) building competitive digital capability; (iii) encouraging investment and implementing the regulatory reform agenda; (iv) ensuring the environmental impact of tourism transport supports growth;

Table 2.1 Travel and tourism total contribution: Australia

Year	2009	2010	2011	2012	2013
Travel and tourism total contribution to GDP (in the past 5 years: 2009–13; USD bn)	95.138	125.59	144.524	151.771	153.406
Travel and tourism total contribution to employment (in the past 5 years: 2009–13 in '000)	1315	1398.3	1373.9	1378.6	1431.4
Travel and tourism total contribution to capital investment (in the past 5 years: 2009–13; USD bn)	12.509	21.932	23.031	24.95	25.767
Travel and tourism total contribution to domestic spending (in the past 5 years: 2009–13; USD bn)	47.97	58.322	70.094	74.113	73.748

Source: WTTC, 2014a.

Table 2.2 **Travel and tourism total contribution: Cambodia**

Year	2009	2010	2011	2012	2013
Travel and tourism total contribution to GDP (in the past 5 years: 2009−13; USD bn)	2.437	2.628	3.318	3.638	4.073
Travel and tourism total contribution to employment (in the past 5 years: 2009−13 in '000)	1485.3	1541.3	1772.8	1805.4	1917.6
Travel and tourism total contribution to capital investment (in the past 5 years: 2009−13; USD bn)	0.242	0.249	0.265	0.325	0.365
Travel and tourism total contribution to domestic spending (in the past 5 years: 2009−13; USD bn)	0.465	0.542	0.695	0.773	0.843

Source: WTTC, 2014a.

(v) increasing the supply of labour, skills and indigenous participation (currently the industry has a labour shortage of 36,000); (vi) building industry resilience, productivity and quality (Tourism Australia, 2011; WTTC, 2014a).

Tourism and hospitality industry: Cambodia

Tourism is Cambodia's third largest industry. Known for its decades of civil war and armed conflicts, the country is regaining its past glory in terms of travel and tourism (Table 2.2). Promoted by its Tourism Department as the 'Kingdom of Wonder', Cambodia is home to over 1800 ancient temples, including one built in the twelfth century. It is a destination for ecological and cultural tourism. With improving flight connectivity, visa exemptions and brand promotion, international tourist arrivals have increased remarkably from 118,183 in 1993 to 2,015,128 in 2007 to 4,200,000 in 2013. Vietnam, China, South Korea, Laos and Thailand are the main sources of tourists. Despite generating US$2.6 billion in revenues in 2013, the OECD (2013, p. 9) notes that there is plenty of room for improvement in certain areas to ensure sustainable tourism. These areas include tourism infrastructure, accommodation, and financial facilities such as automated teller machines (ATMs) that accept Visa cards (*Cambodia Herald*, 2014; Chheang, 2008, 2009; Rodas, 2012).

Tourism and hospitality industry: China

Owing to China's rapidly growing economy, increases in disposable income and consequent growth in domestic tourism, the World Travel and Tourism Council

Table 2.3 Travel and tourism total contribution: China

Year	2009	2010	2011	2012	2013
Travel and tourism total contribution to GDP (in the past 5 years: 2009–13; USD bn)	520.533	559.733	678.836	756.51	864.151
Travel and tourism total contribution to employment (in the past 5 years: 2009–13 in '000)	61981.7	61555	63543.2	63779.2	64412.3
Travel and tourism total contribution to capital investment (in the past 5 years: 2009–13; USD bn)	94.3	78.758	95.521	103.639	116.365
Travel and tourism total contribution to domestic spending (in the past 5 years: 2009–13; USD bn)	288.034	329.916	402.59	454.771	518.008

Source: WTTC, 2014a.

(WTTC) predicts that China is poised to become the world's second largest travel and tourism economy in the world by 2015.

The WTO estimates that 100 million Chinese tourists will travel abroad by 2016. In 2012, Chinese tourists became the world's top international tourism spenders. Recent trend analysis notes that while most Chinese used to travel for shopping now they travel abroad to discover other cultures and learn more about them (Radio Australia, 2014). Known for its contrast between the ancient and modern, China also attracts huge numbers of tourists, with arrivals in 2011 reaching 57.6 million (WTTC, 2014a; Worldwatch Institute, 2013). Chinese tourists are not just going abroad, many are travelling within their own country. Recent records indicate a huge swell in domestic tourism in China. It has reached a point where tourist destinations are experiencing such high inflows – especially during holiday seasons – that they run the risk of becoming uncontrollable, disrupting essential services and having negative impacts on the natural environment, as evidenced by overcrowded tourist spots (Table 2.3).

Tourism and hospitality industry: Hong Kong

Once a British colony, Hong Kong is now the second largest destination for international visitors to the region (Table 2.4). This upsurge in international visitors, the majority from China, is primarily due to implementation of the Individual Visit Scheme (IVS), a visa scheme allowing Chinese residents to visit Hong Kong as

Table 2.4 **Travel and tourism total contribution: Hong Kong**

Year	2009	2010	2011	2012	2013
Travel and tourism total contribution to GDP (in the past 5 years: 2009–13; USD bn)	29.992	36.964	44.033	47.849	50.608
Travel and tourism total contribution to employment (in the past 5 years: 2009–13 in '000)	478.1	521.3	544.6	594.1	594
Travel and tourism total contribution to capital investment (in the past 5 years: 2009–13; USD bn)	4.27	4.384	4.884	5.826	6.569
Travel and tourism total contribution to domestic spending (in the past 5 years: 2009–13; USD bn)	6.415	6.358	7.067	7.609	8.088

Source: WTTC, 2014a.

individuals (Wikipedia, 2013a). It was introduced in 2003 as a strategy to revive tourism in Hong Kong. Prior to this, residents from China could only visit Hong Kong on a business visa or in group tours, but not as individuals.

The WTTC predicts that some 50,061,000 tourists will be visiting Hong Kong by 2023. The tourism industry in Hong Kong is a major contributor to the economy and a key source of jobs for the local workforce. In 2012 it generated 305,500 jobs directly. In earlier decades, when tourism was not commonplace because many of the region's economies were experiencing difficulties and China was closed to the world, Hong Kong took the first mover advantage by investing heavily in infrastructure and establishing itself as the must-go country in Asia for inquisitive European and American tourists. Over the years, Hong Kong has changed its brand image from that of a fishing village in the 1960s to a world-class destination for both leisure and business as well as an international finance centre. In 2011 the Hong Kong Tourism Board (HKTB) initiated the 'Asia's World City' campaign to highlight its cosmopolitan culture. It targeted not only its usual visitor source markets like China, Taiwan and South Korea, but also new ones like India, Russia and the Middle East (HKTB, 2013; SAL, 2008, p. 2; WTTC, 2014c, p. 1).

Tourism and hospitality industry: India

Despite its huge domestic market (30 million Indians travel within India each year), the international tourism sector is booming; yet it accounts for only 1.6 per cent of world tourism revenues. The country – with many places that not only have historical interest but carry the legacy of ancient civilisations – has a long way to go in terms of welcoming overseas tourists. The potential of tourism as a major growth engine and creator of job opportunities is well understood both by the government and the general public. The Ministry of Tourism has taken many initiatives like the *Hunar se Rozgar* ('Create Employable Skills') programme, Incredible India, *Athithi*

Table 2.5 **Travel and tourism total contribution: India**

Year	2009	2010	2011	2012	2013
Travel and tourism total contribution to GDP (in the past 5 years: 2009–13; USD bn)	85.409	104.252	121.78	119.379	137.389
Travel and tourism total contribution to employment (in the past 5 years: 2009–13 in '000)	38145.8	37834.2	39294	39511.9	39420.6
Travel and tourism total contribution to capital investment (in the past 5 years: 2009–13; USD bn)	23.328	28.845	33.091	32.932	37.265
Travel and tourism total contribution to domestic spending (in the past 5 years: 2009–13; USD bn)	55.729	68.315	76.54	76.051	86.506

Source: WTTC, 2014a.

Devo Bhava ('Guests Are God') and the 'Clean India' global brand marketing campaign, as explained in Chapter 3. It has also started promoting India as a 365-day-a-year destination to attract tourists with specific interests and to ensure repeat visits to areas where India has comparative advantage (Table 2.5). Every million rupees invested in tourism creates 47.5 jobs directly and around 85–90 jobs indirectly. In early 2014 the government extended its visa-on-arrival scheme for tourists from 11 to 180 countries with the objective of boosting tourism and achieving its target of nearly doubling foreign tourist arrivals to 12.6 million by 2016. Having implemented all these initiatives, the total market size of the sector is expected to reach US$418.9 billion by 2022 (BBC, 2014; Harish, 2014; IBEF, 2013).

Tourism and hospitality industry: Indonesia

Indonesia boasts popular tourist attractions like Bali, ancient temples and beautiful beaches and attracts a lot of visitors from across the region and beyond. In 2011 it attracted 7.65 million tourists (Table 2.6). Though security has been a major challenge, Indonesia has been steadily welcoming international visitors from Singapore, Malaysia, Australia, China and Japan while arrivals from such countries as the Philippines, Malaysia, India and Germany have been on the increase.

One of the Ministry of Tourism's principal focuses has been on improving the country's infrastructure and its creative economy (by selling unique hand-made

Table 2.6 Travel and tourism total contribution: Indonesia

Year	2009	2010	2011	2012	2013
Travel and tourism total contribution to GDP (in the past 5 years: 2009–13; USD bn)	53.827	64.815	74.999	78.423	87.572
Travel and tourism total contribution to employment (in the past 5 years: 2009–13 in '000)	9271.7	8762.5	8605.5	8909.3	9354.7
Travel and tourism total contribution to capital investment (in the past 5 years: 2009–13; USD bn)	9.734	11.193	13.98	14.985	16.773
Travel and tourism total contribution to domestic spending (in the past 5 years: 2009–13; USD bn)	24.107	29.702	33.711	34.929	38.433

Source: WTTC, 2014a.

artifacts to visitors made by local inhabitants) to facilitate growth in this very important industry. In 2012 the Ministry announced an investment of US$43 billion towards infrastructure development. This is expected to improve connectivity to rural areas as well. In 2011 the Ministry came up with the Master Plan for National Tourism Development whose purpose is to develop and promote 50 national tourism destinations by 2050. With this in mind, it has been promoting tourism through its 'Wonderful Indonesia' campaign since 2011. The purpose of the campaign is to get tourists to appreciate the nation's wonderful nature, wonderful culture, wonderful people, wonderful cuisine and wonderful value for money (GBG, 2013; Wonderful Indonesia, 2013; WTTC, 2014a).

Tourism and hospitality industry: Japan

Japan, the third largest travel and tourism economy in the world, has shown itself to be resilient in the face of natural disasters by welcoming an expected 10 million overseas visitors in 2014 (Table 2.7). Despite being heavily affected by natural disasters – the most recent being the 2011 tsunami and cyclone followed by the nuclear disaster – and the rising value of the Japanese yen, the economy quickly regained confidence with the help of a focussed marketing strategy.

Though business travellers responded well to the Japan National Tourism Organization's (JNTO) Visit Japan campaign, leisure travellers have yet to come back. Japan is looking forward to the 2020 Tokyo Olympic and Paralympic Games and to welcoming many more visitors. Though Japan receives a huge number of tourists from South Korea and China, it has started looking to other countries.

Table 2.7 Travel and tourism total contribution: Japan

Year	2009	2010	2011	2012	2013
Travel and tourism total contribution to GDP (in the past 5 years: 2009–13; USD bn)	336.37	361.205	387.484	399.412	363.113
Travel and tourism total contribution to employment (in the past 5 years: 2009–13 in '000)	4448.8	4363.7	4310.4	4350.7	4267.9
Travel and tourism total contribution to capital investment (in the past 5 years: 2009–13; USD bn)	21.028	27.419	35.163	36.087	32.585
Travel and tourism total contribution to domestic spending (in the past 5 years: 2009–13; USD bn)	202.54	213.94	228.942	233.907	211.752

Source: WTTC, 2014a.

For instance, the Ministry of Tourism (government of India), the Japan Tourism Agency and the Ministry of Land, Infrastructure, Transport and Tourism (government of Japan) have recently signed a Memorandum of Understanding with the following objectives: to encourage citizens to travel to each other's country; exchange information and data related to tourism; encourage cooperation between tourism stakeholders such as hotels and tour operators; establish exchange programmes for cooperation in HR development; exchange visits from tour operators/media/opinion makers to promote two-way tourism; exchange experiences in the areas of promotion, marketing, destination development and management; participate in travel fairs/exhibitions in both countries; and promote safe, honourable and sustainable tourism (*Express TravelWorld*, 2014; JNTO, 2013; Timetric Research, 2013; WTTC, 2012).

Tourism and hospitality industry: Korea, South

South Korea, Asia's fourth largest economy, has been struggling recently. However, the tourism sector outperformed other industry sectors and helped revive the overall economy (as shown in Table 2.8). Interestingly, the reason for such a large number of tourists has been attributed to Korean pop sensation Psy's viral music video *Gangnam Style* (Naidu, 2013).

Tourism revenues hit a record high in 2012 with more than 10 million people visiting the country. Most tourists come from Japan, China, Taiwan and Hong Kong, respectively. To keep up the momentum, the Korea Tourism Organization (KTO) is looking towards other potential markets like India where it has targeted 100,000 arrivals for 2013. In 2013, the industry contributed US$68 billion to the economy and created 1.6 million jobs (KTO, n.d.; Niyogi, 2013; WTTC, 2014b).

Table 2.8 **Travel and tourism total contribution: Korea, South**

Year	2009	2010	2011	2012	2013
Travel and tourism total contribution to GDP (in the past 5 years: 2009–13; USD bn)	52.623	57.202	61.342	66.769	71.345
Travel and tourism total contribution to employment (in the past 5 years: 2009–13 in '000)	1542.4	1432.5	1441.1	1583.8	1573.3
Travel and tourism total contribution to capital investment (in the past 5 years: 2009–13; USD bn)	5.76	6.308	6.813	6.883	7.472
Travel and tourism total contribution to domestic spending (in the past 5 years: 2009–13; USD bn)	30.285	35.592	38.523	40.22	44.028

Source: WTTC, 2014a.

Table 2.9 **Travel and tourism total contribution: Malaysia**

Year	2009	2010	2011	2012	2013
Travel and tourism total contribution to GDP (in the past 5 years: 2009–13; USD bn)	36.041	40.685	43.346	47.41	52.227
Travel and tourism total contribution to employment (in the past 5 years: 2009–13 in '000)	1768.3	1707.3	1600.3	1708.6	1795.4
Travel and tourism total contribution to capital investment (in the past 5 years: 2009–13; USD bn)	3.52	4.605	5.13	6.099	6.578
Travel and tourism total contribution to domestic spending (in the past 5 years: 2009–13; USD bn)	11.536	12.98	15.471	16.739	18.296

Source: WTTC, 2014a.

Tourism and hospitality industry: Malaysia

Tourism has always been a key economic driver in Malaysia. It is the sixth largest contributor to gross national income and third largest foreign exchange earner for the country (Table 2.9).

The government recognises the potential of this industry and has identified tourism as a national key economic area (NKEA) in its mega-plan to become a high-income country by 2020. As part of the government's 'Visit Malaysia 2014' campaign, it lined up multiple tourism products like home staying [home staying is a form of tourism and/or study abroad that allows a visitor to rent a room from a local family in a homelike setting (Rivers, 1998)], contemporary art tourism and shoe festivals. The country is expecting 28 million foreign tourists in 2014. Most visitors come from Singapore, Indonesia, China (including Hong Kong and Macau), Thailand, Brunei, India, Philippines, Australia, Japan and the UK, respectively. In order to maximise return on investment, Malaysia has got together with Indonesia in a multi-country—multi-destination joint promotion, a package offering tourists the opportunity to visit three heritage sites in each of the two countries. It also has a huge domestic market of 131 million visitors (as of 2011) (Department of Statistics Malaysia, 2012). According to the WTTC, tourism employs over 1.7 million people (*Brisbane Times*, 2014; MOTM, 2013; WTTC, 2014).

Tourism and hospitality industry: Myanmar (Burma)

'Let the Journey Begin' was the first image-building initiative launched by Myanmar in 2013 (Table 2.10). Now that the country has a more democratic regime, the government has made the development of tourism a national priority.

The government believes its development is essential for economic growth and poverty reduction. Between 2011 and 2012, for the first time in its history, Myanmar received in excess of a million international visitors. According to WTTC estimates, in 2012 the industry directly created 293,700 jobs and indirectly another 735,000 jobs in other parts of the economy. The country's newly gained political stability, improved connectivity and visa relaxation have made it possible for

Table 2.10 **Travel and tourism total contribution: Myanmar (Burma)**

Year	2009	2010	2011	2012	2013
Travel and tourism total contribution to GDP (in the past 5 years: 2009–13; USD bn)	1.24	1.516	1.644	1.794	1.97
Travel and tourism total contribution to employment (in the past 5 years: 2009–13 in '000)	675.7	665.9	684.3	711.4	734.9
Travel and tourism total contribution to capital investment (in the past 5 years: 2009–13; USD bn)	0.102	0.1	0.107	0.115	0.125
Travel and tourism total contribution to domestic spending (in the past 5 years: 2009–13; USD bn)	0.812	1.002	1.108	1.196	1.311

Source: WTTC, 2014a.

tourists from around the world to visit this emerging tourist destination, one that is rich in cultural and natural heritage. Thailand, China, Japan, the US, South Korea, France, Malaysia, Singapore, the UK and Germany are the key sources of foreign tourists. The Ministry of Hotels and Tourism (MOHT) Myanmar has developed a master plan (funded by the government of Norway) that envisages a high target of 3.01 million international visitors by 2015 and 7.48 million by 2020. Broadly, the plan outlines six strategic programmes: strengthening the institutional environment; building HR capacity and promoting service quality; strengthening safeguards and procedures for destination planning and management; developing quality products and services; improving the connectivity and tourism-related infrastructure and building the image, position and brand of tourism (MOHT, 2013; WTTC, 2014a).

Tourism and hospitality industry: New Zealand

Tourism is New Zealand's second largest export industry. The industry directly employs 5.7 per cent of the workforce or 110,800 full-time equivalent employees, so is integral to its economy (Table 2.11).

Though there has been steady growth in visitor arrivals, the majority from Australia and China (excluding Hong Kong and Macau) followed by the US, the UK and Japan, the Tourism Ministry is concerned about a decrease in tourist spending. The industry employs more than a third (36 per cent) of its employees part-time compared with 19 per cent of all New Zealand workers. It is also facing the challenge of maintaining labour productivity. As part of its destination marketing, the government is investing heavily in tourism to improve productivity and eliminate barriers to innovation arising from a skills shortage. For instance, it has decided to invest NZ$10 million annually into the Major Events Development Fund to increase the number and quality of such events. As part of an integrated strategy to boost its tourism industry, the government has also been marketing and promoting international education by targeting markets like China and India (MBIE, 2013; WTTC, 2014a).

Table 2.11 Travel and tourism total contribution: New Zealand

Year	2009	2010	2011	2012	2013
Travel and tourism total contribution to GDP (in the past 5 years: 2009−13; USD bn)	18.071	20.253	23.903	24.914	25.274
Travel and tourism total contribution to employment (in the past 5 years: 2009−13 in '000)	418.9	415.4	434.8	426.4	430.1
Travel and tourism total contribution to capital investment (in the past 5 years: 2009−13; USD bn)	1.065	1.421	2.487	2.72	2.791
Travel and tourism total contribution to domestic spending (in the past 5 years: 2009−13; USD bn)	8.238	9.474	10.634	11.427	11.411

Source: WTTC, 2014a.

Table 2.12 Travel and tourism total contribution: Philippines

Year	2009	2010	2011	2012	2013
Travel and tourism total contribution to GDP (in the past 5 years: 2009–13; USD bn)	12.55	13.129	15.177	17.556	19.523
Travel and tourism total contribution to employment (in the past 5 years: 2009–13 in '000)	2864.1	2628.2	2766	2910.7	3028.4
Travel and tourism total contribution to capital investment (in the past 5 years: 2009–13; USD bn)	1.61	1.364	1.382	1.521	1.688
Travel and tourism total contribution to domestic spending (in the past 5 years: 2009–13; USD bn)	4.332	4.664	5.384	6.037	6.867

Source: WTTC, 2014a.

Tourism and hospitality industry: Philippines

Tourism has been identified by the Filipino government as a major pillar in the Medium Term Philippine Development Plan (MTPDP), a development framework involving many strategies, policies, programmes and activities for sustainable growth and development of the country (Table 2.12).

'It's more fun in the Philippines' is the tagline used by the Department of Tourism (DOT) to let tourists know what to expect during their visit to the country. Despite natural disasters, domestic political uncertainty and other challenges, 4,681,307 foreign visitors, representing a year-on-year growth of 9.56 per cent, visited in 2013. South Korea, the US, Japan, China, Australia, Singapore, Taiwan, Canada, Hong Kong, the UK, Malaysia and Germany are the top source countries, respectively. Hopes are high of reaching the DOT target of 10 million international arrivals by 2016 and as a result generating 7 million jobs. With this objective in mind, many initiatives have been launched including the DOT's 'Tourism Star Philippines', a new set of awards starting in September 2014. The awards consist of two categories aimed at recognising the contributions of (a) tourism front-liners and individuals who embody the true Filipino brand of warm hospitality and go the extra mile in the service of tourists; and (b) local chief executives (LCEs), such as mayors or governors, who devise projects that contribute positively to the tourism industry (DOTP, 2014; WTTC, 2014a).

Tourism and hospitality industry: Singapore

Tourism plays a major role in the economy supporting over 160,000 jobs (Table 2.13). Strategically located at the heart of Southeast Asia, Singapore is the

Table 2.13 Travel and tourism total contribution: Singapore

Year	2009	2010	2011	2012	2013
Travel and tourism total contribution to GDP (in the past 5 years: 2009–13; USD bn)	18.053	23.072	28.564	30.708	31.968
Travel and tourism total contribution to employment (in the past 5 years: 2009–13 in '000)	203.7	238.3	267.8	291	295.6
Travel and tourism total contribution to capital investment (in the past 5 years: 2009–13; USD bn)	10.9	11.598	13.013	13.278	13.79
Travel and tourism total contribution to domestic spending (in the past 5 years: 2009–13; USD bn)	4.385	5.074	5.87	6.605	7.028

Source: WTTC, 2014a.

gateway to the East. Despite its small domestic market, it welcomed over 14 million international visitors for the first time in its history in 2013.

Indonesia, China, Malaysia, Australia and India are the top-five visitor source markets. The Singapore Tourism Board (STB), the statutory body overseeing all aspects of tourism, is responsible for devising strategies to keep up the momentum. For instance, it aims to protect its base of key source markets; it plans to invest to grow source markets like Japan and Vietnam that fall just outside its key source markets; and it plans to pursue niche opportunities for less explored markets like the Gulf States and Russia. The country regularly develops tourism products and keeps its workforce fully updated to cope with them. Its well-thought-out funding system encourages industry players to tap into funds like the Tourism Product Development Fund and Training Industry Professional in Tourism (TIP-iT) schemes to benefit from and be part of the country's economic growth story. Singapore was named Asia's Top Convention City for the 12th consecutive year in 2014. In 2010 it changed its tagline from 'Uniquely Singapore' to 'Your Singapore' to personalise tourist visits. Innovative tourism products, good infrastructure, a trained workforce and safe environment combine to make this dynamic country a tourism hotspot (Loh, 2010; STB, 2013; WTTC, 2014a).

Tourism and hospitality industry: Sri Lanka

Having consigned its civil war to the past, Sri Lanka is portraying itself in a new light with its 'Refreshingly Sri Lanka' slogan. The country welcomed 650,000 visitors in 2010, the highest number of tourist arrivals in recent history, and is looking forward to attracting more than 4 million tourists by 2020 (Table 2.14).

The government's vision for the future of the industry is based on sustainable development and includes protection of the environment and distribution of economic benefits to a larger cross section of society. As part of a 5-year strategy, the

Table 2.14 Travel and tourism total contribution: Sri Lanka

Year	2009	2010	2011	2012	2013
Travel and tourism total contribution to GDP (in the past 5 years: 2009–13; USD bn)	3.46	4.258	5.176	5.284	6.106
Travel and tourism total contribution to employment (in the past 5 years: 2009–13 in '000)	568.8	598.6	635.9	663.1	672.5
Travel and tourism total contribution to capital investment (in the past 5 years: 2009–13; USD bn)	0.493	0.538	0.637	0.632	0.715
Travel and tourism total contribution to domestic spending (in the past 5 years: 2009–13; USD bn)	1.315	1.638	1.941	1.972	2.227

Source: WTTC, 2014a.

government envisages a number of key objectives for the target year of 2016: (a) increase tourist arrivals from 650,000 in 2010 to 2.5 million; (b) attract US$3 billion in foreign direct investment (FDI); (c) increase tourism-related employment from 125,000 in 2010 to 500,000 and expand tourism-based industries and services across the island; (d) distribute the economic benefits of tourism to a wider cross section of society and integrate tourism with the real economy; (e) increase foreign exchange earnings from US$500 million in 2010 to US$2.75 billion; (f) contribute towards improving global trade and economic linkages; (g) position Sri Lanka as the world's most treasured island for tourism. The country has a two-pronged strategy to enhance tourism. By setting up Domestic Tourism Units to collect statistical information, it hopes to gain a better understanding of current and prospective tourists. It is also seeking cooperation from the Sri Lankan diaspora and missions abroad to reach out to newer markets such as America, East Asia, the Middle East, Eastern Europe and Australasia (MED, 2011; WTTC, 2014a).

Tourism and hospitality industry: Taiwan

Ever since the country opened up to visitors from mainland China in 2008, there has been an upsurge in tourist arrivals (Table 2.15). Taiwan welcomed 7 million international tourists in 2012, 1.97 million of whom were from China and in excess of one million from Japan. Taiwan has seen an increase in the number of domestic trips made by its residents, which in 2011 was 152.27 million.

The government has catered to the increasing demands of tourism by heavily investing in its infrastructure such as building hotels and renovating accommodation facilities. The Industrial Development Bureau and the Central Region Office (both of the Ministry of Economic Affairs) initiated the Tourism Factory Project in 2003, launched to improve both tourism and manufacturing. The project highlights various products manufactured in Taiwan and organises guided tours for tourists interested in

Table 2.15 **Travel and tourism total contribution: Taiwan**

Year	2009	2010	2011	2012	2013
Travel and tourism total contribution to GDP (in the past 5 years: 2009–13; USD bn)	15.361	20.808	23.91	24.174	24.886
Travel and tourism total contribution to employment (in the past 5 years: 2009–13 in '000)	417.6	527.6	590.3	605.1	597.9
Travel and tourism total contribution to capital investment (in the past 5 years: 2009–13; USD bn)	3.89	4.815	5.12	4.981	5.392
Travel and tourism total contribution to domestic spending (in the past 5 years: 2009–13; USD bn)	12.202	15.049	16.106	16.024	16.79

Source: WTTC, 2014a.

visiting manufacturing facilities to have first-hand experience of the famous 'Made in Taiwan' product label. The government recently announced its target of welcoming '10 million tourists' by 2015. With this objective in mind, it came up with a new slogan, 'Taiwan – the heart of Asia'. It has also found innovative ways to attract tourists. For instance, the Tourism Bureau's Taiwan Giveaways app is aimed at attracting Americans to Taiwan. Unlike conventional vouchers, this app (worth in excess of US$100) includes information about: (a) sights and shops that rank high in the not-to-be-missed lists of CNN Travel, Flavorwire.com and the Daily Meal; (b) a city tour of Taipei; (c) free gifts like Taiwan's specialty pineapple cakes, Taiwanese tea and relaxing neck massage; and (d) buy-one-get-one-free offers on selected items and services (MOFAT, 2013; Sun Ten, n.d.; WTTC, 2014a; *Xinhua*, 2013).

Tourism and hospitality industry: Thailand

According to the WTTC, tourism is a major pillar of Thailand's economy with tremendous growth prospects (Table 2.16). The country's tourism slogan 'Amazing Thailand: It Begins with People' is an attempt to portray the country as a popular and welcoming tourist destination. The WTTC expects tourism's direct contribution to GDP to grow by an average 6.8 per cent per year between 2012 and 2022.

Despite political unrest and natural disasters, Thailand was ranked 9th in the region in the World Economic Forum (WEF)'s tourism and travel competitiveness index (TTCI) in 2013, a year in which Thailand welcomed a record number of foreign tourists (over 26.5 million). China, Malaysia, Russia, Japan, South Korea and India are the top source countries (TDN, 2014; WEF, 2013).

Tourism and hospitality industry: Vietnam

The slogan 'Vietnam – Timeless Charm' accurately portrays the country's many World Heritage cultural sites and natural wonders (Table 2.17). As in other

Table 2.16 Travel and tourism total contribution: Thailand

Year	2009	2010	2011	2012	2013
Travel and tourism total contribution to GDP (in the past 5 years: 2009−13; USD bn)	42.899	45.991	55.79	60.967	66.967
Travel and tourism total contribution to employment (in the past 5 years: 2009−13 in '000)	4921.5	4268.1	4354.6	4818.7	5273.1
Travel and tourism total contribution to capital investment (in the past 5 years: 2009−13; USD bn)	7.01	4.866	6.129	7.314	8.664
Travel and tourism total contribution to domestic spending (in the past 5 years: 2009−13; USD bn)	10.893	12.734	14.225	15.265	16.676

Source: WTTC, 2014a.

Table 2.17 Travel and tourism total contribution: Vietnam

Year	2009	2010	2011	2012	2013
Travel and tourism total contribution to GDP (in the past 5 years: 2009−13; USD bn)	9.466	10.272	11.971	12.973	14.566
Travel and tourism total contribution to employment (in the past 5 years: 2009−13 in '000)	4025.6	4096.7	3939	3892.1	4033.7
Travel and tourism total contribution to capital investment (in the past 5 years: 2009−13; USD bn)	2.958	3.211	3.45	3.718	4.029
Travel and tourism total contribution to domestic spending (in the past 5 years: 2009−13; USD bn)	3.591	4.187	4.653	4.899	5.6

Source: WTTC, 2014a.

countries in the region, tourism is a key pillar of the economy, on which in excess of 2 million direct jobs depend. The Ministry of Culture, Sports and Tourism has taken a three-pronged marketing approach to promoting sustainable tourism.

With the objective of balancing the economic, social and environmental aspects of tourism, the Ministry has targeted: (a) attracting 10−10.5 million international visitors, serving 48 million domestic tourists and increasing tourism revenue to US$18−19 billion by 2020; (b) increasing the numbers employed in tourism to over 3 million (870,000 of which are direct jobs), ensuring tourism development contributes to the preservation and promotion of Vietnam's cultural values and improving the lives of its people; and (c) developing green tourism by preserving and promoting the value of natural resources and environmental protection. China, Japan, South Korea, Russia and Australia are the key source markets for Vietnam. While growing stably and welcoming 3.54 million foreign tourists in 2013, it faces a number of challenges regarding infrastructure development, training HR, innovative product development and rising cost of labour (TITC, 2013; WTTC, 2014a).

Summary

The above clearly shows that the tourism and hospitality industry is key to the region's economy. Infrastructure, newer products, brand image of countries in the region, political stability, connectivity and well-coordinated strategies all play major roles in attracting both foreign and domestic visitors.

Retail industry

Retail is the service industry connecting producers and consumers. It not only sells goods to consumers but also provides them with services like after-sales services. Growth in the retail industry is often driven by the economic growth of a country, the supply and demand of goods and services, proper infrastructure, as well as good governance and regulations. Tables 2.18−2.19 depict comparative data of retail sales as a proportion of GDP in 2011 (per cent of GDP), retail sales as a proportion of consumer spending (per cent of consumer expenditure) and employment in retail as a proportion of national employment 2007−12 (per cent share), respectively.

These data clearly demonstrate that retail contributes significantly to a country's economy. China is ranked fifth for retail globally but among the focus countries had the highest percentage of retail sales as a proportion of consumer expenditure. In contrast, Vietnam is ranked fourth for retail globally but had the highest retail sales as a proportion of GDP. With the exception of a few countries, the industry is growing across the region. However, each country has its own distinct situation, issues and challenges. The state of the retail industry across the region and how the retail landscape is changing are given in the following sections.

Table 2.18 **Retail sales data**

Country	Retail sales as a proportion of consumer expenditure (% of consumer expenditure)		Retail sales as a proportion of GDP: 2011 (% of GDP)	
	2011	Global rank	2011	Global rank
Australia	27.8	43	15.29	43
Cambodia	NA	NA	NA	NA
China	43.5	5	17.37	35
Hong Kong	28.1	42	18.4	32
India	30	38	16.93	37
Indonesia	25.3	47	13.9	46
Japan	36.8	12	21.64	13
Korea, South	30.5	36	16.02	40
Malaysia	22.2	51	11.46	51
Myanmar (Burma)	NA	NA	NA	NA
New Zealand	35.6	16	20.39	16
Philippines	33.7	28	24.47	6
Singapore	22.1	52	8.24	52
Sri Lanka	NA	NA	NA	NA
Taiwan	34	26	19.79	20
Thailand	35.6	17	20.71	15
Vietnam	36.1	14	25.28	4

Source: Euromonitor International from national statistics, 2013.

Table 2.19 **Employment in retailing as a proportion of national employment 2007–12**

Country	Employment in retailing as a proportion of national employment 2007–12 (% share)					
	2007	2008	2009	2010	2011	2012
Australia	11.7	11.22	11.18	10.56	9.97	9.63
Cambodia	NA	NA	NA	NA	NA	NA
China	3.84	3.84	3.8	3.76	3.75	3.77
Hong Kong	6.58	6.73	6.76	6.99	7.03	7.26
India	9.78	9.93	9.84	9.89	9.84	9.92
Indonesia	11.43	11.39	11.42	11.33	11.29	11.27
Japan	11.83	11.83	11.91	11.75	11.86	11.9
Korea, South	6.42	6.35	6.47	6.51	6.48	6.52
Malaysia	2.6	2.94	2.97	3	3.02	3.08
Myanmar (Burma)	NA	NA	NA	NA	NA	NA
New Zealand	11.11	10.49	10.71	10.85	10.46	10.59
Philippines	9.17	9.38	9.45	9.53	9.69	10.09
Singapore	5.16	5.52	5.83	6.01	5.99	5.93
Sri Lanka	NA	NA	NA	NA	NA	NA
Taiwan	12	11.73	11.67	11.53	11.39	11.54
Thailand	5	5	4.93	5.12	5.29	5.51
Vietnam	10.6	11.65	11.51	11.35	11.33	11.63

Source: Euromonitor International from national statistics, 2013.

Retail industry: Australia

There are almost 140,000 retail businesses in Australia. They make a significant contribution to economic output and in 2009–10 generated AU$53 billion (4.1 per cent of GDP). Employing over 1.2 million people, the industry is one of Australia's largest employers. However, overall slowing of the economy, consequent decrease in disposable incomes, increase in online retailing and intensified competition from global retailers are some of the key challenges facing the industry (PC, 2011).

Retail industry: Cambodia

Retail is still mostly traditional in Cambodia with small family-owned shops and wet markets (i.e., fresh meat and produce). Despite the industry gradually picking up momentum as a result of economic growth and increases in disposable incomes, this is mainly restricted to Phnom Penh, the country's capital. In excess of US$1.5 billion was made available to the wholesale and retail sectors in 2010, equal to 50 per cent of total loans granted by the commercial banks. Despite international investors especially from Japan and Hong Kong showing interest in investing, the business environment is constrained by corruption, poverty and lack of infrastructure leading to high electricity and land cost (Cunningham, 2011; EIU, 2013; USDOC, 2011).

Retail industry: China

Turning over US$1.8 trillion in retail sales in 2009, China is the second largest retail market in the world and the largest retail market in the region. Growth, rises in household incomes and an Internet-savvy middle class of over 200 million make the country an interesting market; all the more interesting in that the retail market is composed of many small and medium-sized retailers. There were about 2400 foreign-invested retail enterprises and very few inter-provincial retailers as of 2009. The reason for this is believed to be high market entry barriers. In contrast, online retailing also known as 'e-tailing' (i.e., electronic retailing) has grown in leaps and bounds and is predicted to reach US$650 billion by 2020. The government initiative to promote e-tailing and digital consumption is a means of facilitating their contribution to GDP. However, retail's sharp increase is not devoid of challenges, which range from an over-supply of shopping malls to fast-changing consumer behaviour, significant increases in operating costs, and logistics bottlenecks (Austrade, 2013; FBIC, 2013; Sheng and Zhao, 2010).

Retail industry: Hong Kong

Retail is very important to Hong Kong's economy. There are 64,000 retail establishments (as of 2012) employing over 320,000 and contributing heavily to GDP. In recent years, however, retail sales have been slowing down due to spending by Mainland Chinese tourists declining. Rising rental costs are also putting pressure on retailers. In the current situation strong growth in Internet retailing is expected as it will help reduce operational costs and at the same time provide benefits to consumers (Azar, 2013; EABFU, 2013).

Retail industry: India

Retail in India has a turnover of more than US$500 billion, which is expected to increase to US$865 billion by 2015 as a result of the middle class growing from over 21 million households in 2011 to an estimated 91 million by 2030, whereas the domestic retail market is projected to be turning over US$1.3 trillion by 2020. Since the potential is so great, the government has started many initiatives, encouraging not only domestic retailers but also foreign investors. For instance, in 2013 it liberalised policies to permit foreign retailers to open stores in cities with a population of less than one million (previously there had to be more than one million). India has the third largest Internet user base in the world (with over 74 million users) and is also making strides in online retailing, a sector that is expanding at a very fast pace. However, the industry has a number of challenges to deal with, like shortages of skilled HR, policy barriers and red tape, prominence of the unorganised retail sector, and the non-availability of sophisticated real estate.

Retail industry: Indonesia

Retail is one of Indonesia's largest industries when it comes to employment. It consists of 10.3 million establishments, mainly composed of small (2.3 million) and micro (7.9 million) establishments. International brands are just starting to make their mark. Economic growth, a large pool of middle-class consumers and increases in domestic demand were responsible for retail sales of US$12.75 million in 2013. With strong domestic demand, rising competition between retailers, infrastructure development and use of technology, the industry is undergoing major change (Dyck et al., 2012; Kurniawan, 2014).

Retail industry: Japan

Though Japan is the second biggest retail market in the world, declining birth rates and an ageing population have resulted in the number of people per household dropping, which has a knock-on effect on retail by lowering the levels of consumption. There has been a sharp decline in the number of retail stores from 1.72 million in 1982 to 1.13 million in 2007. However, its rich senior citizens have rallied to the call and have been spending millions to help the industry (Flath and Nairu, 1992; JETRO, 2007).

Retail industry: South Korea

The retail industry in South Korea presents a mixed picture. Home to the world's largest retail store (Shinsegae Centumcity Department Store, occupying 3.163

million square feet of floor space), the industry is grappling with the challenges of inflation, lowering consumer confidence and low sales figures. Interestingly, it is well ahead of most of the region in terms of the fast-growing online retail sector as a result of it having a high penetration of Internet and digital-savvy consumers. Retail sales are expected to reach US$318.57 billion by 2015. Though the retail landscape is dominated by *chaebols* (diversified conglomerate family-controlled firms characterized by strong ties with government agencies; Rowley, 2013), inter-national retailers have also established bases in the country. Domestic retailers have expanded locally and some have ventured into such overseas markets as China, Indonesia and Vietnam (PwC, 2011; Sternquist and Jin, 1998).

Retail industry: Malaysia

The retail sector in Malaysia is driven both by domestic demand and spending by tourists. According to a recent forecast, retail sales are expected to touch MYR94.4 billion by 2015. The increase in tourist arrivals (25 million visited in 2012) has boosted the retail industry. Tourists spent US$2.6 billion on shopping in 2012, although the rising cost of living has affected domestic demand. New highs are expected as a result of the 'Visit Malaysia 2014' tourism promotion (*The Business Times*, 2013; *The Star Online*, 2014).

Retail industry: Myanmar (Burma)

Retail in Myanmar has a turnover of US$13.2 billion. It is dominated by traditional forms of retail (90 per cent of the market value) consisting of small shops. The modern retail market, like supermarkets and convenience stores, represents the remaining 10 per cent of the market value and is only found in urban locations. The country, which is undergoing democratic reform, is expected to prosper in the com-ing years and the retail industry to grow exponentially (IM, 2012; Thwe, 2013).

Retail industry: New Zealand

Much interest has been shown in the retail industry in New Zealand. Overall, the performance of the country's 32,978 stores (as of 2012) has been consistent as a result of the growth of tourism. According to recent statistics, over a third of tourist spending (US$7.9 billion as of 2012) is on retail sales. Yet, margin erosion of net profit before tax over the past few years has been significant (from 6.3 per cent in 2003 down to 3 per cent in 2013). A decrease in the number of high-spending tourists is given as the reason (NZRA, 2013).

Retail industry: the Philippines

With economic growth and increases in domestic consumption, the retail industry in the Philippines is on a stable growth path. Foreign investment gradually increased after the Retail Trade Liberalization Law was passed in 2000.

Modernisation and increased demand for foreign brands have added to the growth of the industry in recent years. *Business Monitor International* predicts retail sales to grow from US$32.17 billion in 2012 to US$36.31 billion by 2016. The challenge is to keep up the momentum by integrated use of technology in the industry (Deloitte, 2013a,b; Digal, 2001).

Retail industry: Singapore

The retail industry in Singapore is a key contributor to the economy. Complementing the growth in tourism, the retail industry comprises 19,700 establishments. They generate about SG$37.4 billion in sales and employ about 120,600. Increased hiring costs as a result of tighter labour market conditions is a challenge facing the industry, prompting it to look at automating business processes (e.g., using robots to help in cooking that include stir-frying vegetables with their automated robotic arms and taking orders from customers) to improve business growth and productivity (DOS, 2014; PME Jobs Network, 2012).

Retail industry: Sri Lanka

It is early days for the retail industry in Sri Lanka. The war-affected country has yet to make its mark. According to a recent survey, Sri Lanka was deemed one of the most promising markets for retail sector growth in the region. There were 924,500 people employed in the wholesale and retail trade in 2008, making it the third largest employment sector. Local firms dominate the retail industry, as foreign investment has yet to take off (RAM, 2012).

Retail industry: Taiwan

The retail industry in Taiwan has a turnover of US$333.7 billion and is a major contributor to the economy. With the highest convenience store density in the world, Taiwan had 638,577 firms in the wholesale and retail trade industry in 2012, employing around 1,747,000. Its young, tech-savvy retail consumers are the highest online spenders in the Asia Pacific. The huge increase in the number of Chinese tourists as a result of visa relaxation — allowing independent travellers to enter the country — is a key reason for the growth of the retail sector. Retail has attracted much foreign investment in recent years, reaching US$1.018 billion in 2012 (Mishkin, 2012).

Retail industry: Thailand

Political uncertainty in Thailand has affected consumer confidence and impacted its retail industry. Despite increases in tourist arrivals in recent years and the government's economic stimulus initially boosting the industry's performance, decreases in domestic demand and lowering consumer confidence have negatively affected the industry. The Retail Association has urged the government to waive tariffs on imported goods and promote a value-added tax refund at the point of purchase to encourage foreign tourists to shop more in Thailand (*Bangkok Post*, 2014; Rungfapaisarn, 2013).

Retail industry: Vietnam

Vietnam's economic growth coupled with rising middle-class incomes are not only helping the industry to grow, but to become one of the world's fastest growing retail markets. The increasingly young population is significantly impacting the industry. As of 2012 there were 90 million people less than 25 years old. People in this age group are more interested in modern retail forms like supermarkets, hypermarkets, minimarts and convenience stores, although traditional wet markets are not only prevalent but deemed part of society. After Vietnam opened its door to foreign-owned retail business in 2009, local retail companies expanded to build a more vibrant distribution network. The Vietnam Retail Association was established in 2007 to promote the retail industry and strengthen the development of Vietnamese distribution services by linking Vietnamese retailers (USDA/FAS, 2013).

Summary

Competition amongst retailers has intensified as a result of globalisation and changing consumer behaviour and expectations. Overall, it can be seen that retail is closely linked to the tourism and hospitality industry and that much of retail sales depends on visitor spending. Technology use in the industry in the region has had the effect of bringing consumers and sellers closer together.

Healthcare industry

Healthcare involves the provision of goods and services to deliver curative (to cure a disease or medical condition), preventive (to prevent disease), rehabilitative (to diagnose, treat and manage people with disabling medical conditions) and palliative (to relieve and prevent patient suffering) care to patients (Wikipedia, 2013b). Healthcare is one of the world's largest and fastest growing industries, with total revenues of about US$2.8 trillion (CII, 2014).

Table 2.20 shows the extent to which the healthcare industry contributes to economies in the region. The industry has huge growth potential because many key parameters (listed in the table) fall short of Organisation for Economic Co-operation and Development (OECD) averages. For instance, with the exception of Australia, all others in the region had practising physicians well below the OECD average of 3.1 per thousand people in 2010. Recent years have witnessed an upsurge in medical tourism, in which consumers cross borders to avail themselves of healthcare facilities. Also known as medical travel, health tourism or global healthcare, 'medical tourism' is a term initially coined by travel agencies and the

Table 2.20 **Healthcare in the greater Asia Pacific (GAPAC) countries**

Country	Health expenditure, total (% of GDP), 2011	Health expenditure per capita (current US$), 2011	Medical resources and usage (as of 2011)		Life expectancy at birth, total (years), 2011	Fertility rate, total (births per woman), 2011	Population ages 65 and above (% of total), 2011	Age dependency ratio (dependents to working age population), 2011
			Physicians (per 1000 people)	Hospital beds (per 1000 people)				
Australia	9	5939	3.9	3.9	82	1.9	14	48
Cambodia	5.7	51	0.2	0.7	71	2.9	5	58
China	5.2	278	1.8	3.8	75	1.7	9	36
Hong Kong	5.1	#	1.8	5.1	83	1.2	13	34
India	3.9	59	0.6	NA	66	2.5	5	54
Indonesia	2.7	95	0.2	0.6	70	2.4	5	53
Japan	9.3	3958	2.1	13.7	83	1.4	24	58
Korea, South	7.2	1616	2	10.3	81	1.2	11	37
Malaysia	3.6	346	1.2	1.8	75	2	5	47
Myanmar (Burma)	2	23	0.5	NA	65	2	5	45
New Zealand	10.1	3666	2.7	2.3	81	2.1	13	51
Philippines	4.1	97	NA	1	68	3.1	4	63
Singapore	4.6	2286	1.9	2.7	82	1.2	9	36
Sri Lanka	3.4	97	0.5	NA	74	2.3	8	49
Taiwan	NA	NA	NA	NA	NA	NA	NA	NA
Thailand	4.1	202	0.3	2.1	74	1.4	9	39
Vietnam	6.8	95	1.2	2.2	75	1.8	7	42

Source: World Bank, 2013c.

mass media to describe this rapidly growing practice. Tourism and healthcare are both beneficiaries of this practice. Medical tourism is expected to grow 30 per cent annually. The region boasts well-known destinations for medical tourism (e.g., Singapore for diagnostics of cancer and India for cardiology and orthopaedics; MED, 2013; ReportLinker, 2014; Shah, 2011; *The Economist*, 2011a). The healthcare industry of each of our focus countries is presented in the following sections.

Healthcare industry: Australia

Healthcare in Australia is provided by both private and government institutions. It is a booming industry and has the highest per capita expenditure in the region. In 2010–11 the healthcare and social assistance industry, to give it its full title, employed some 1.3 million or 11.4 per cent of total employment, more than any other sector in the country (ABS, 2012; World Bank, 2013c).

Healthcare industry: Cambodia

Healthcare in Cambodia is still in a nascent phase, and there is huge scope for development. The country's health expenditure per capita is one of the lowest as is its ratio of physicians per thousand people. Poverty and lack of infrastructure are the main impediments to growth (World Bank, 2013a).

Healthcare industry: China

China's healthcare industry is well on the way to booming as a result of huge domestic demand. International investors are ready to set up camp and explore opportunities, even in traditional Chinese medicine. China spent 5.2 per cent of GDP on healthcare in 2011 and hopes to be spending somewhere between 8 and 9 per cent by 2020. However, external investors with limited understanding of local laws and government regulations will find the industry complex and a challenge (Wharton School, 2007; World Bank, 2013c).

Healthcare industry: Hong Kong

The healthcare landscape in Hong Kong is changing. There are three main factors impacting the industry: an ageing population that is constantly increasing, balancing capital expenditure to deliver international class facilities and reducing operational costs. In 2013 the government allocated US$2.54 billion to the Hospital Authority to help improve primary and community care. The government is focussed on building new assets and improving existing facilities in an effort to improve the industry (GLD, 2010; Prosser, 2013; World Bank, 2013c).

Healthcare industry: India

A major contributor to the economy, healthcare in India is expected to grow to US$158.2 billion in 2017 from US$78.6 billion in 2012. The availability of quality treatments at a much lower cost than in many advanced Western nations, R&D facilities, a growing middle class with disposable income seeking high-quality healthcare facilities and the growing medical tourism market all add to the rapid growth of India's healthcare industry. However, shortages of medical professionals (0.6 per thousand people), the need for infrastructure development and greater awareness of health and hygiene especially in rural areas are some of the challenges that need to be addressed (CII, 2014; PTI, 2013; World Bank, 2013c).

Healthcare industry: Indonesia

Growth in the economy, increasing incomes and a growing middle class are fuelling the development of healthcare in Indonesia. Despite many challenges, such as poor medical conditions and shortages of medical professionals, in 2014 the country made the significant decision to roll out universal healthcare and provide health insurance to its 250 million people within 5 years. Indonesia's expenditure on healthcare is predicted to reach US$60.6 billion in 2018 (Bellman, 2014; World Bank, 2013c).

Healthcare industry: Japan

Despite healthcare statistics (such as longest life expectancy in the world) painting a positive picture, an ageing population that is constantly increasing, low fertility rates and natural disasters have put a strain on the industry in Japan. There are acute shortages of GPs and specialists which impact the overall cost of healthcare driven by the rules of supply and demand. Moreover, higher concentration of physicians in larger urban areas than rural areas is adding to high inequality in physician distribution in Japan. Though the system of *kaihoken* (health insurance for all) has been prevalent for all residents in Japan for more than the last 50 years, out-of-pocket expenses have increased due to the rising healthcare costs. Thus, to balance the impact of rising healthcare cost on one hand and acute shortages of GPs on the other, the government regulates the market and every two years sets fees (takes cost control measures) for all healthcare services. The fees are set by negotiations between the Health Ministry and physicians. The Health Ministry then publishes a list of prices for medical services and products applicable for its residents. (Henke and Kadonaga, 2009; Toyabe, 2009; Wikipedia, 2012; World Bank, 2013c).

Healthcare industry: South Korea

Healthcare in South Korea is booming. Despite the country having an ageing population that is rapidly increasing and one of the world's highest suicide rates, the overall health indicators are positive with US$1616 spent per capita in 2011, though there is still scope for improvement in areas like number of physicians per thousand people, which at 2 is much below the OECD average of 3.9. The government plans to expand its medical workforce by recruiting foreign doctors. The government is focussing on cost management to deal with its healthcare challenges. In 2012 South Korea signed a free trade agreement (FTA) with the US that will eliminate 95 per cent of both nations' healthcare tariffs within 5 years. South Korea is also aiming to capitalise on medical tourism. To this end the government recently set itself a target of attracting one million foreign patients by 2020 and the Ministry of Health and the Korea Health Industry Development Institute collaborated on a project to improve the country's medical policy and infrastructure for foreign patients. Most medical tourists come from the US and China (Walsh, 2012; World Bank, 2013c).

Healthcare industry: Malaysia

Healthcare in Malaysia is undergoing development and is primarily driven by domestic demand. However, the country has woken up to the tremendous economic potential posed by healthcare, especially in the medical tourism area, in addition to looking after the well-being of its people. There were 130 public sector and 210 private sector hospitals in 2010. The country aims to create medical tourism opportunities, products and services and by 2020 to welcome one million health travellers. Japan is one of Malaysia's target markets for health tourism. The Ministry of Health plans to conduct 1000 clinical trials and generate approximately 181,000 new jobs in the industry by 2020 (Carvalho, 2013; MOHM, 2010).

Healthcare industry: Myanmar (Burma)

Healthcare in Myanmar is in serious need of reform. According to a 2013 World Health Organization (WHO) report, Myanmar came last in a list of 190 countries regarding overall health system performance. The country spends just 2 per cent of GDP on healthcare. Corruption and dysfunctional operation of the industry are challenges that need to be addressed for the industry to grow further (Shobert, 2013; World Bank, 2013c).

Healthcare industry: New Zealand

Healthcare in New Zealand is a major contributor to the economy. In 2011 per capita health expenditure was US$3666, one of the highest in the region. Healthcare services are made available through public and privately funded services. There are in excess of 220 hospitals in New Zealand (MTANZ, n.d.).

Healthcare industry: the Philippines

Healthcare in the Philippines has been volatile, to put it mildly. In 2005 the Asian Development Bank (ADB) awarded a grant of US$1 million to support health sector reform and thereby improve the efficiency of public health service delivery.

However, the ensuing years saw the country grapple with political change and concomitant uncertainty, resulting in a further decline in the healthcare industry. In 2010, for example, about 200 hospitals went bust and a further 800 partially shut down. Healthcare workers have migrated in droves to other countries, which has made the situation worse by adding to the fragility of the industry (ADB, 2005; Barcelona, 2010; World Bank, 2013c).

Healthcare industry: Singapore

The healthcare industry in Singapore comprises both public and private healthcare and is one of the most advanced in the region. In 2011 the industry had over 3000 healthcare establishments and 40,000 practising registered healthcare professionals. With plans to build new healthcare facilities, the country is looking to recruit 20,000 healthcare workers by 2020. As a result of an ageing population that is increasing in numbers, there is growing impetus to increase healthcare spending, which is projected to be SG$12 billion a year by 2020, up from SG$4 billion in 2011 (Austrade, 2014; Contact Singapore, 2014).

Healthcare industry: Sri Lanka

Healthcare in Sri Lanka is dominated by the public sector and most of its facilities are publicly funded. Private healthcare services are gradually making their mark, however. As a result of an ageing population that is on the increase, the prevalence of non-communicable diseases (such as cancer, heart disease and asthma) is on the rise. Despite healthcare expenditure significantly increasing in recent years, the industry has had to deal with inherent shortages of skilled HR, including qualified medical professionals (RAM, 2013).

Healthcare industry: Taiwan

Taiwan's 20,000 primary care units and 500 secondary care units are not enough to meet the demands of its ageing population, the increasing prevalence of chronic disease, rising healthcare costs and decline in the number of hospitals (from 617 in 2000 to 508 in 2010). The healthcare industry is seriously in need of a boost (PwC, 2012; World Bank, 2013c).

Healthcare industry: Thailand

Thailand has one of the lowest ratios of physicians per thousand people in the region. Although the prospects for medical tourism are good, political instability, rising death rates and high entry barriers are key challenges the industry has to address (World Bank, 2013c).

Healthcare industry: Vietnam

In recent years the Ministry of Health in Vietnam has made efforts to revamp the healthcare industry. In 2008 it allocated US$1 billion to improving the infrastructure and upgrading the industry. However, shortages of skilled medical professionals, many of whom left the profession to join non-medical fields as a result of unattractive pay packages and poor infrastructure, are one of the key challenges facing the industry (Sanjeed, 2009; World Bank, 2013c).

Summary

Ageing populations, increases in life expectancy, rising incomes and tendencies to spend more on healthcare facilities are key factors in making the healthcare industry the region's largest and fastest growing. Despite improvements being made in the development of innovative products over the years, the industry is struggling with an acute shortage and take-up of medical resources. In the coming years, the healthcare industry in the region will have little choice but to look again at such issues and challenges if growth is to be sustained.

Education industry

The education industry covers all aspects of teaching, training and research played out in schools, colleges, universities and various private institutions. It is a key contributor to economies and can be used as a measure of the well-being of a country. Global expenditure on education in 2012 was US$4,450.90 billion (EconomyWatch, 2010; GSV, 2012). Internationally, education is characterized by three trends: (a) student mobility; (b) programme mobility such as distance education and online education; (c) institution mobility where domestic institutes partner with others overseas to deliver programmes, etc. Table 2.21 provides key statistics on education in our focus countries. Since e-learning has become an important trend in the education industry, we take a closer look at the Internet penetration of countries in the region as well as the region's Internet users.

Education industry: Australia

Australia's education industry is growing fast and is the country's third largest export industry. Each year the industry attracts more than 450,000 students from about 200 countries. Australia is currently ranked fifth in the world list of top providers of international education services. In 2009 there were 27,622 enterprises in the industry, employing 804,547 people and contributing AU$17.2 billion (around 36 per cent of total service exports) to the country's export income. The top-three markets for education-related travel services are China, India and South Korea. Growth in online education as well as a growing number of branch

Table **2.21 Education industry key statistics**

Country	Total public expenditure on education (as a % of total government expenditure) as of 2010	Education expenditures (% of GDP) (as of 2010)	Literacy rate (as of 2012)	Internet users (per 100 people) as of 2012
Australia	12.9	4.5	99	82.3
Cambodia	12.4	1.7	73.6	4.9
China	11.4 (1999)	1.9	92.2	42.3
Hong Kong	20.2	3.9	93.5	72.8
India	10.4	3.2	61	12.58
Indonesia	17.1	3.6	90.4	15.36
Japan	9.4	3.5	99	79.05
Korea, South	15.8	4.6	97.9	83.8
Malaysia	18.9	6.2	88.7	65.8
Myanmar (Burma)	4.4	1.2	89.9	1.06
New Zealand	16.1	6.2	99	89.51
Philippines	15	2.5	92.6	36.2
Singapore	10.3	3.7	92.5	74.18
Sri Lanka	8.1	NA	91.2	18.2
Taiwan	20.18	NA	96.1	NA
Thailand	22.3	4.2	92.6	26.5
Vietnam	19.8	1.8	94	39.49

Source: CIA World Factbook, 2012.

campuses are current trends. However, the strong Australian dollar and high cost of living and studying in Australia have posed challenges to growth of the industry (DFAT, 2011; Invest in Australia, 2013).

Education industry: Cambodia

The education industry in Cambodia is on a stable growth path. Despite poverty being the reality for students opting out of schools, the country has been able to achieve a literacy rate of 73.6 per cent. In 2001 the first Education Strategic Plan 2001−05 was adopted, its objective was to reform the education system. This was followed by the National Education for All Action Plan (in 2003); its target is for all children to receive education by 2015. The three guiding policies of the Education Strategic Plan are: making access to education services fair, improving the quality and efficiency of education and strengthening institutional capacity to deliver on education. While progress has been slow, the industry has gradually improved in terms of efficiency, effectiveness as well as institutional and capacity development. Education features prominently in the country's broader national strategy known as the 'Rectangular Strategy', whose objectives are to enhance economic growth, employment as well as equity and social justice. The strategy highlights 'strengthening the quality of education' as an important aspect of 'capacity building and human resource development', something that is essential for the target to be achieved (UNICEF, 2011; World Bank, 2013a).

Education industry: China

Education has played a significant role in China for centuries. Huge economic growth, increases in disposable incomes, higher investment in industry by the government and huge domestic demand are all factors that depend on education. Widespread illiteracy is commonly given as an obstacle to modernisation of the country. Hence, the government emphasises the importance of students having at least nine years of compulsory education. Today, China has a literacy rate of 92.2 per cent. In 2010 there were 23 million students enrolled in colleges and universities. China has been encouraging upskilling of its workforce through private training to meet the demands of the growing economy. Each year nearly 100 million people receive some form of training through 20,000 registered, yet fragmented, private training institutions. In recent years China has also been focussing on modernising education by utilising information and communication technologies (ICT) to facilitate teaching, learning, educational management and other related activities. In 2012 the number of Internet users in China was truly vast (42.3 per cent of the entire population) – an indication of the success of its booming online education industry. However, the industry is grappling with several challenges, such as quality of education, unclear roles and responsibilities of governments and schools, disparity between the demand for quality education and the availability of skilled and qualified teachers (Deloitte, 2013b; Hall and Lewis, 2008; *People's Daily*, 2001).

Education industry: Hong Kong

In order to position itself as a knowledge-based business hub, the Hong Kong government has heavily invested in educational reform – be it secondary, higher, vocational or continuing. The government is also promoting internationalisation and web-based learning. In the recent past representatives from the Education Bureau (EDB; the government body responsible for education policies) and various institutions visited countries like China, India and the UK to facilitate collaboration and exchange programmes. Education gets the largest share of government expenditure. In 2014 the government allocated US$8.61 billion to education. Shortage of HR, mismatch of skills for industry requirements, severe land shortages, low birth rates and consequent low enrolments are key challenges facing the industry. Endowment funds have been established by the government to support the Qualifications Framework (QF). Launched in 2008, the QF provides a transparent and accessible platform to promote life-long learning and enhance the competitiveness of the workforce. This seven-level hierarchy orders and supports the qualifications of the academic, vocational and continuing education sectors and is underpinned by a robust quality assurance mechanism. It aims to help people set clear goals and directions for continuous learning to obtain quality-assured qualifications.

Education industry: India

India's education industry is somewhat of an enigma. On the one hand, the country has 36 per cent of the world's illiterate adult population (283 million); on the other hand, it churns out hundreds of thousands of graduates every year. India has 367 universities, 18,000 colleges, about 0.5 million teachers, and 11 million pupils. The industry is growing at an astounding pace and is expected to turn over US$97 billion in 2015. The industry is comprised of both government and private players. The Ministry of Human Resources Development (MHRD) is in charge of accreditation and quality assurance. India is expected to have the largest workforce in the world by 2030. There is huge potential in the country for adult and continuing education, as evidenced by increasing demand. With the increase in Internet penetration, the online education market is also expected to turn over US$40 billion by 2017.

Education industry: Indonesia

There are 144,228 elementary schools, 28,777 junior high schools, 10,765 senior high schools, 49 public universities and numerous private training providers in Indonesia. The country spends over 17 per cent of the national budget on education. Indonesia allows foreign educational institutions or training providers to run businesses in the country provided they partner with a local company that acts as an agent and runs the business in Indonesia for them. However, over the years international interest in its education industry has declined, especially when compared with neighbouring economies like Singapore and Malaysia. There are a number of reasons for this ranging from its huge population, lack of proper infrastructure and qualified HR to regional disparity. In order to cope with such challenges, Indonesia has initiated funding and scholarships to encourage promising higher education students from low-income families (GBG, 2012; UKTI, 2013).

Education industry: Japan

Despite the industry being expected to grow overall, the rapid increase in Japan's ageing population and declining numbers of younger people have had a negative impact. In 2010 there were 53,185 educational institutions in Japan including elementary, lower secondary, upper secondary and university. These numbers are dwindling as many fail to fill their student quotas and opt to close or merge with institutions finding themselves in the same boat or with foreign universities. The lack of quality research work and the high incidence of bullying at schools are fuelling distrust in the education system. The US and the UK are the traditional destinations for Japanese students wanting to get a degree overseas. Although this trend is gradually changing, the acquisition of English language skills remains important to many people (Ken Research, 2012; NZT&E, 2007).

Education industry: South Korea

The education industry in South Korea has progressed by leaps and bounds in the past few decades, achieving a 97.9 per cent literacy rate in 2012, up from just 22 per cent in 1945. Over the years the country has invested heavily in education in the knowledge that it is key to economic prosperity. Its teenagers rank second in the world for mathematics skills, just behind Finland. The country also boasts a huge population base proficient in using new technology. Internet penetration in 2012 had reached 83.8 per cent of the population. Nevertheless, the high costs of tuition and lack of jobs for the majority of its graduates are a cause of growing concern for the industry (BBC News, 2005; Ken Research, 2013; *The Economist*, 2011b).

Education industry: Malaysia

Malaysia spends nearly 19 per cent of the national budget on education, which employs 6.7 per cent of the total workforce. As of 2009 there were 20 public universities, 20 private universities, 13 university colleges, more than 300 colleges, 27 public polytechnics, 5 branch campuses of foreign universities and 63 community colleges. Malaysia attracts international students from many countries, but primarily from China, Indonesia, Iran, Nigeria and Bangladesh. However, the government has concerns about the alignment of education with human capital development. It plans to develop education as an export industry, upskilling the workforce and developing Malaysia as an education hub in Asia. The government recognises the country needs a critical mass of researchers to be globally competitive. In 2008 it launched the 'MyBrain15' initiative with the objective of producing 60,000 Malaysian PhD graduates by 2020. The government has been encouraging higher education institutions to focus on R&D in such areas as biotechnology and tropical medicine (Loke, 2011).

Education industry: Myanmar (Burma)

As soon as Myanmar became a democracy, the country initiated a new phase of socioeconomic development in which education was given priority. Myanmar spends just 1.2 per cent of the national budget on education. According to a 2008 survey conducted by UNICEF, three of every ten primary school-aged children did not attend any school and all curricula and course material had to be approved by the military. The country needs to make changes at the system level for the education industry to reach a minimum standard (Curriculum Project, n.d.).

Education industry: New Zealand

The education industry in New Zealand is a major contributor to the economy. There were 422,000 students enrolled in formal study programmes in 2012 and 139,000 in workplace-based learning. The industry is highly developed and well on par with global standards. In an effort to boost skills and employment, in 2012 the government set a target for 85 per cent of 18-year-olds to achieve an NCEA[1] level 2 or an equivalent qualification by 2017 and 55 per cent of the population aged 25 to 34 years a level 4 or higher qualification by 2017. The country spends over 16 per cent of the national budget on education. Education is New Zealand's fifth largest export industry and by 2012 was turning over NZ$2.6 billion. China, India, Korea and Japan are the top-four countries for the export of education services. The country plans to double the industry's turnover to NZ$5 billion (US$4.1 billion) by 2025. Shortages of faculty and competition from Asian countries who are fast upgrading their capabilities are challenges that need to be addressed (MOE-NZ, 2009).

Education industry: the Philippines

The education industry in the Philippines is in a pretty dismal state. Despite the government spending over 17 per cent of the national budget on education in 2010, instructional material/textbook shortages, underpaid but overworked teachers and lack of infrastructure including classrooms are common features of the industry. Despite the country producing in excess of 35,000 teachers each year, they find the challenges too great and many look for opportunities abroad, specifically in the US, China, Japan and the Middle East. The result is a brain drain and acute shortages of teachers.

Education industry: Singapore

Singapore is widely recognised as the education hub of the East. A proponent of life-long education, the country boasts a quality infrastructure, skilled professionals and innovative curriculum. The government spends over 10 per cent of the national budget, amounting to SG$11.6 billion (FY2013), on education. The country exports education expertise in the areas of content delivery, curriculum development, teacher training, assessment and standards and industry skills training to many countries, but primarily to China, India, the Middle East and Southeast Asia. In recent years Singapore has placed even more emphasis on maintaining the quality standards of the education industry. For instance, to raise the standards of private education institutions (PEIs), the Private Education Act was introduced to: ensure a basic level of protection for students, including safeguarding course fees; raise the quality of providers to meet a minimum standard in their academic processes and corporate governance; and improve access by consumers to information on providers and courses. To further improve the status of the industry, the government has taken many other initiatives ranging from process innovation and HR development to increasing the number of publicly funded university places from 13,000 to 16,000 by 2020. As part of process innovation, the government encouraged PEIs to use ICT by adopting school management systems to raise their productivity, achieve better cost efficiencies and enhance the learning experience of students (IE Singapore, 2013; MOE-S, 2013).

Education industry: Sri Lanka

Sri Lanka has set a target of achieving excellence in higher education by 2020. Yet, the key challenge is to improve its education profile by substantially boosting participation in basic education, achieving universal primary completion and improving the quality of education. The World Bank awarded Sri Lanka a US$60 million grant to help develop its education industry. The grant was to: (a) promote equitable access to basic education and secondary education; (b) improve the quality of education; (c) enhance the economic efficiency and equity of resource allocation and distribution within the education system; and (d) strengthen education governance and service delivery (UNESCO, 2009; World Bank, 2013b).

Education industry: Taiwan

The education industry in Taiwan has undergone massive changes. At the beginning of the 1990s, reform took place in the form of liberalisation and diversification of education. This was an extension of social reform, and higher education became accessible not only to the elite, but also to the masses. Over the years, policies like the 'Popularisation of Education' and the 'Cultivation of Technical Persons' were introduced; they had a long and positive influence on Taiwan. By 2012 there were 11,495 educational institutions. Nevertheless, there are a number of challenges the industry needs to address, such as incompatibility between academic curricula and market demands, sudden large increases in student enrolment and the resultant pressure on academic faculty and HR, making it difficult for universities to maintain the high academic quality of the past (MOE-C, 2013).

Education industry: Thailand

There are over 37,000 educational institutions and 20 million students in Thailand, 2.2 million of whom are in the higher education sector. The industry is dominated by public sector institutions and organisations. They form 82 per cent of the industry; the remaining 18 per cent are private institutions. Growth of the industry is held back by a range of factors from weaknesses in teacher training and support programmes, poorly educated parents, disadvantaged populations to iodine deficiencies in children. However, the government realises the importance of education for economic development. The National Economic and Social Development Plan identified four pillars to underpin the education industry: (a) increase the focus on quality of education; (b) improve teachers' capabilities; (c) modernise schools and learning centres; (d) improve educational management (MOE-T, 2008; World Bank, 2011).

Education industry: Vietnam

The education industry has been given priority in Vietnam. It attracts nearly 20 per cent of the national budget, an increase from 14 per cent in 1997 and 18.6 per cent in 2005. It has made plans to improve educational quality and efficiency as a means of achieving its national goal of economic well-being. Vietnam has come a long way since 1945 when the government issued a document entitled *An Illiterate Nation Is a Powerless One.* The slogan bandied about today is 'Education for All' – a goal targeted to be achieved by 2015. Though funds, proper infrastructure and qualified people have been in short supply, Vietnam has been able to attain a literacy rate of 94 per cent, much higher than countries with a similar economic status. In recent years the government has focussed on improving quality standards in education. It has applied checks and measures on student intakes and closed many private institutions not meeting quality standards. Despite the growing economy, increasing disposable incomes and some of the above factors, many Vietnamese students have opted to study abroad. In 2012 there were some 106,000 Vietnamese students studying in 49 foreign countries and territories. The US, Australia, Singapore, China and Taiwan are the five most popular overseas destinations (Clark, 2013; World Bank, 2006).

Summary

The education industry prepares human resources (HR) for all other industries. The countries in the region have recognised its significance as a means of improving other industries. The GAPAC is a paradox in itself – on the one hand, it is home to most of the world's illiterates while, on the other hand, its education industry helps produce some of world's most significant innovative products and services. However, the bottom line is there remains much to be done and industry players will have to work hard at improving quality to stay ahead.

Security industry

The security industry is defined by the United Nations as 'a broad term used to describe the structures, institutions and personnel responsible for the management, provision and oversight of security in a country.' It is generally accepted to include defence, law enforcement, corrections, intelligence services and institutions responsible for border management, customs and civil emergencies. Those parts of the judicial sector responsible for the adjudication of cases relating to alleged criminal conduct and misuse of force are in many instances also included. Furthermore, the industry includes actors that play a role in managing and overseeing the design and implementation of security, such as ministries, legislative bodies and civil society groups. Other non-state actors that could be considered include customary[2] or informal authorities and private security services.

Today, the global security industry, including private security, turns over in excess of US$1.7 trillion. Interestingly, recent statistics note that private security forces outnumber the police 2:1 worldwide and that globally there are in excess of 20 million private security guards. The private security industry is growing at the rate of 7.4 per cent a year and is expected to turn over US$244 billion globally by 2016 (PI, 2011).

Table 2.22 details military expenditure in the GAPAC, gives an overview of the police forces in the region and provides information on the black market value of

Table 2.22 Key security statistics

Country	Military expenditure (% of GDP) as of 2012	Military expenditure (% of central government expenditure) as of 2012	Size of national police forces (as of year)	Police officers per 100,000 inhabitants	Total country black market value (in US$ billion)
Australia	1.71	6.5	49,242 (2009)	217	14.62
Cambodia	1.54	13.2	64000 (2012)	428	0.614
China	2.01	NA	1,600,000 (2007)	120	261
Hong Kong	NA	NA	27,117 (2007)	393	NA
India	2.41	15.2	1,585,353 (2013)	130	68.59
Indonesia	0.78	NA	579,000 (2012)	243	23.05
Japan	0.99	5.1	251,939 (2006)	197	108.3
Korea, South	2.8	NA	93,600 (2004)	195	NA
Malaysia	1.54	7.1	102,000 (2012)	370	2.99
Myanmar (Burma)	NA	NA	93,000 (2012)	154	1.704
New Zealand	1.1	2.4	11,000 (2012)	247	NA
Philippines	1.19	7.3	149,535 (2014)	138	17.27
Singapore	3.51	26.6	40,000 (2012)	752	0.2693
Sri Lanka	2.42	13.6	89,000 (2012)	438	NA
Taiwan	2.2	16.2	NA	NA	2.608
Thailand	1.47	7	230,000 (2012)	344	13.95
Vietnam	2.15	NA	NA	NA	0.8155

Sources: Havocscope, 2014; SIPRI, 2012; Wikipedia, 2014; World Bank, 2012.

the region. The three countries in the region with the highest black market value are China, Japan and India. China, Cambodia and Vietnam all doubled their military spending between 2004 and 2013, whereas Singapore's military expenditure was among the highest in the region (26.6 percent of national budget was spent in 2012). The global military and security industry research firm Stockholm International Peace Research Institute (SIPRI) identifies military expenditure as all current and capital expenditure on:

- the armed forces, including peacekeeping forces;
- defence ministries and other government agencies engaged in defence projects;
- paramilitary forces, when judged to be trained and equipped for military operations;
- military space activities including military and civil personnel (retirement pensions of military personnel and social services for personnel), operations and maintenance, procurement, military research and development, and military aid (the military expenditure of the donor country) but excluding civil defence and current expenditure on previous military activities (such as veterans' benefits, demobilisation, conversion and weapon destruction; SIPRI, 2012; UN, 2012).

Security industry: Australia

Australia recently conducted a study to evaluate the cost of crime. In addition to tangible or monetised costs, such as medical expenses, loss of income as a result of injury and government costs such as the criminal justice system, intangible costs such as quality of life and losses incurred because of fear of crime were taken into account. By 2010 it was estimated that the average cost of crime (all assaults) was AU$2,093 per assault or nearly AU$36 billion a year, equalling approximately 4.1 per cent of GDP. However, this figure is lower than the US (AU$26,206 per assault) and the UK (AU$9,872 per assault). Australia spends 1.71 per cent of GDP on its military. Total expenditure on the criminal justice system can be broken down as: the police with 72 per cent, corrective services with 22 per cent and criminal court administration with 6 per cent. In 2005 the police force comprised 58,167 police staff (excluding the Federal Police) or 286 police officers per 100,000 persons. The government spends AU$289 for every person in Australia. Apart from military and police organisations, over 5000 security and investigative businesses are registered in Australia, and over 110,000 licenses are issued to individuals or companies. The private security market is dominated by five companies. The industry has been growing steadily, especially in areas like electronic surveillance and monitoring and cash in transit. In many cases the police and the private security industry work together. However, there are concerns about infiltration and exploitation of the private security industry by organised crime groups trying to gain access to firearms, licensed premises, major events and public and private assets. Therefore, quality control in the provision of licences is vital to the industry (AIC, 2010; Prenzler et al., 2009; SIPRI, 2012; Webber, 2010; World Bank, 2012).

Security industry: Cambodia

Cambodia's security challenges are mainly external and relate to disputes over territorial sovereignty. Some 13.2 per cent of the national budget is spent on the military. Despite the country having one of the highest ratios of police officers per 100,000 inhabitants (at 428), approximately 70 private security companies work hand in hand with the police. Internal security suffers from a lack of proper infrastructure and skilled HR, poverty and corruption. For instance, according to a recent report released by the International Labour Organization (ILO), 10 per cent of the country's GDP (amounting to US$1.7 billion) is lost to corruption each year (B2B Cambodia, n.d; Chheang, 2013; Havocscope, 2014).

Security industry: China

Like many other industries in China, the security industry is growing at a tremendous pace. The country spends 2.1 per cent of GDP on the military. The ratio of 120 police officers per 100,000 citizens is complemented by a growing private security force. The private security industry emerged in the 1980s with government assistance. There are over 18,000 companies and almost one million employees in the industry. Many of these companies own what is called a 'well-known trademark', which allows them to enjoy multi-class protection in the Chinese trademark system. China recognises that technological innovation is critical to providing advanced security services. The Security Technology and Risk Assessment Key Laboratory of the Ministry of Public Security was set up to encourage product innovation in the industry. The industry is undergoing a consolidation phase with frequent mergers and acquisitions. Nevertheless, the absence of clear national legislation about how the industry should function, lack of effective management and the availability of counterfeit security products are key challenges that need to be addressed (CSPIA, 2012; Jing and Ghosh, 2009).

Security industry: Hong Kong

The imprisonment rate in Hong Kong is one of the highest in the region (163 per 100,000 in 1999). The percentage of female prisoners is one of the highest in the world. The country boasts the sixth highest police-to-population ratio in the region (393 police officers per 100,000 inhabitants in 2007) and a large private security force. The private security industry consists of over 700 companies employing over 160,000 personnel. In recent years the industry focus has been on the increase in technology-related crime such as online business fraud. The challenge is to keep security industry personnel updated with new technology competencies (APCCA, 1999; Broadhurst, 2000).

Security industry: India

After the Mumbai attack, questions were raised about the state of security in the country. Though India spends 2.41 per cent of GDP on the military and is a nuclear power, in many cases the safety and security of its people are compromised. Its dismal police-to-population ratio of 1 per 761 points toward the need for reform. The hiatus had led to rapid development of the private security industry. With approximately 5 million private security guards and 15,000 companies (both unorganised and organised) operating in this field, the private security industry is expected to grow at a rate of 40 per cent per annum. There are many challenges facing the industry, such as concerns about compliance, lack of availability of skilled HR, lower use of technology, talent retention due to lack of proper career progression paths and lack of proper legislation regarding the rights and duties of private security guards (DNA India, 2013; FICCI, 2013).

Security industry: Indonesia

Indonesia is facing both internal and external challenges, including religious violence, ideological tension, political conflict and international terrorism. Though security is of major concern, its defence budget is one of the lowest in the region. Nevertheless, its military consists of 317,273 army, 62,556 navy and 33,900 air force personnel. The general environment of insecurity has helped the private security industry grow; in 2006 there were in excess of 200,000 private security guards in the country. Lack of infrastructure (low Internet penetration) and skilled HR are key challenges that need to be addressed (BICC, 2006; Sukma, 2013).

Security industry: Japan

The security industry in Japan is undergoing major change. The geopolitical situation of Japan and the rising number of crimes (over 2.5 million per annum) have prompted the country to look again at the policies and strategies used to cope with both its external and internal security challenges. In 1999 the private security industry comprised in excess of 8000 security companies and employed 350,000 personnel. Currently, there are almost double the number of private security guards as there are police officers. The plan to rent out private drones that take off when intruder alarms are tripped and record footage of break-ins as they happen is evidence of the sophistication of private security companies. However, there is an acute shortage of trained HR, as recently pointed out by a government panel on information. Some 80,000 information security professionals are needed to protect key IT systems from attack. Despite 265,000 personnel in the workforce, 160,000 of them need further training to get up to scratch (Muncaster, 2013; Phys.org, 2012; Yoshida and Leishman, 2006).

Security industry: South Korea

The security industry in South Korea has been growing at an annual rate of more than 20 per cent. The Security Industry Act 2001 provides guidelines regarding the roles and responsibilities of a security manager and a security officer, the activities they may perform, and the training requirements and licensing criteria of a security company. The act requires each security guard to undergo monthly in-house training and refresher training in subjects such as the Security Services Industry Act, crime prevention, terrorism countermeasures, self-defence, information security, marksmanship and explosives disposal. Though South Korea plays a major role in the manufacture of security devices and has huge domestic demand, it has only 1.7 per cent of the global market. The challenges that need to be addressed include improving training, dealing with false alarms, improving the character and quality of security HR, improving security technology, legal issues, private investigations, the relationship between private security officers and police officers (Button, 2006; Song, 2009).

Security industry: Malaysia

The MH730 and MH17 airliner disasters have prompted Malaysia to revisit its security industry policies and strategies. Until recently the country's outlook towards security was what Tang (2011) called 'cautious optimism'. Territorial security is maintained by one of the smallest militaries in the region (109,000 in 2009). Malaysia is not party to any alliance or military pact. Malaysia's internal security challenges are controlled by a police force and 667 security companies with a workforce of 130,000 (Tang, 2011; *The Malaysian Insider*, 2012).

Security industry: Myanmar (Burma)

Post the 2011 political reform and change of government, the security industry in Myanmar is undergoing a new growth phase. The country has to control both domestic security threats (like intra-state ethnic clashes) and cross-border security challenges (specifically with Thailand and Bangladesh). The country's national police force, which numbers 93,000, and the mostly unorganised private security industry have an uphill task ahead of them to ensure the country's security and sovereignty.

Security industry: New Zealand

The New Zealand security industry turns over NZ$2.8 billion and comprises 1440 security companies employing in excess of 14,000 private security guards. The industry recently underwent a major reform that specified compulsory licensing and training requirements for a wider range of security-related activities. The need for a dedicated enforcement body (incorporating the Complaints, Investigation and Prosecution Unit) has been proposed (Cosgrove, 2008; NZSA, n.d.).

Security industry: the Philippines

The military personnel of the Philippines in 2010 numbered around 115,000 (made up of 65,000 army, 35,000 navy and 15,000 air force personnel). There were 149,535 police officers in 2014 and over 400,000 personnel working for over 1200 private security companies. Industry change has been on the agenda of the government since the mid-1980s. A recent report identified 'performance deficit' as one of its key challenges. Recently, the government in partnership with the UN developed a Security Sector Reform Index (SSRI) to generate a baseline on the state of security governance in the country. The Philippines' close relationship with Canada facilitates the acquisition of security equipment and expertise. Improving defence planning systems, operational and training capacity, logistics provision, HR development, personnel management, financial controls and strategic communications are key challenges that need to be addressed (ISDS, 2011; Ramos, 2009).

Security industry: Singapore

Singapore is one of the safest countries in the region. Nearly 27 per cent of the national budget is spent on the military, and spending on homeland security amounts to US$200 billion per year – one of the highest in the region. A police force of almost 40,000 officers is backed up by more than 200 companies in the private safety and security industry employing 35,000 personnel. The Security Industry Regulatory Department (SIRD) of the Singapore police force regulates the private security industry and ensures the quality of its HR. The industry is a good example of the success of public–private partnerships. To train and educate people for the industry, in 2006 the Ministry of Manpower (MOM) launched a competency framework – the Singapore Workforce Skills Qualifications System for the Security Industry (Security WSQ). The Security Association Singapore (SAS) helped the MOM to develop the WSQ. The Security WSQ assesses, recognises and equips individuals with the relevant competencies required for a job in this industry. However, the level of management expertise, female participation and long working hours are key challenges that need to be addressed (Chee, 2010; Interpol, n.d; WDA, 2012).

Security industry: Sri Lanka

The security industry in Sri Lanka played a major role both in the civil war and in the post-ceasefire era. Issues and challenges range from lack of management, poor infrastructure, to growth of the unorganised sector staffed by untrained and unskilled HR. Interestingly, Sri Lanka's security and justice institutions employ one of the region's largest numbers of women. The private security industry (both organised and unorganised) is growing at a rapid pace. The 250 registered private security agencies employ in excess of 70,000. This number excludes, of course, the large number of people employed in the unorganised sector (lankanewspapers.com, 2006; Pavey and Smith, 2009).

Security industry: Taiwan

Externally, falling defence expenditure (from 3.8 per cent of GDP in 1994 to 2.1 per cent in 2012) has raised concerns regarding the preparedness of the military.

Internally, the wealth gap, lack of skill development and demographic changes with an ageing population increasing in number are some of the major socioeconomic changes impacting on security. High-profile crimes and the basic insecurity of the people have triggered a booming private sector industry that turned over in excess of US$3 billion in 2008 (BBC News, 2011; Samedi, 1997).

Security industry: Thailand

Repeated military coups, failed coup attempts and civil unrest make the country a testbed for the security industry. Thailand has a sizeable pro-monarchist military (306,600 in 2009) and police force (344 police officers per 100,000 inhabitants). Rising social unrest has brought about a situation in which the private security industry has rapidly grown. Made up of about 3000 primarily small operators, they employ in excess of 400,000 staff. The quality standards of most of these private security firms are yet to be tested. As a result of high demand for these services, many smaller companies often resort to employing poorly paid and poorly trained Burmese migrants (Chambers, 2014; Kittikanya, 2005; Tang, 2011).

Security industry: Vietnam

Despite there being few known internal security challenges, rising border conflicts with China have been a concern. Vietnam is one of several countries in the region that doubled military spending between 2004 and 2013 and built up its armed forces, estimated to number about 5 million. Security is one of the priority industries and, according to recent estimates, one in six working people (approximately 43 million) are employed either full time or part time in the industry (Ghosh, 2013; Thayer, 2012).

Summary

Security in all its forms is a fundamental human need. With the prevalence and sophistication of criminal activities increasing worldwide, the industry has become one of the fastest growing in both the region and beyond. To cope with growing demand, structured government security industries and private and somewhat unstructured security agencies exist side by side. There is a pressing need for the government to formulate legislation to maintain the quality standards of the industry, train skilled security forces and look for ways to restrict/control criminals trying to enter the industry.

Energy industry

The word 'energy' is derived from the Latin word *energia* meaning activity or operation. The energy industry consists of the production and sale of energy as well as fuel extraction, manufacturing, refining and distribution. Its significance for the growth and development of an economy cannot be overstated. A country's energy reserves determine the wealth and economic prowess of that nation. Energy reserves are the quantities of energy sources (such as coal, gas or oil) that could be recovered with presently available technology at an economically viable cost. It is calculated on the basis of geological data and future projections. The industry is highly regulated and mostly controlled by government departments responsible for energy security. Energy security is defined as the adequate, reliable and affordable provision of energy to support the functioning of the economy and social development with minimal supply disruptions at a price that does not affect the competitiveness of the economy and encourages investment in the sector. The energy industry has to balance energy supply and efficient usage at an optimal cost against carbon emission reduction. The region has a huge contribution in the dynamics of global energy. Table 2.23 illustrates the relevant energy industry statistics of the region (Australian Government, 2009; Harper, 2007). The energy industry of each of our focus countries is presented in the following sections.

Energy industry: Australia

Australia is energy rich and was the world's ninth largest energy producer in 2011. The high-quality energy resources, mostly owned by the government, make the industry a significant contributor to the economy. Owing to the increase in population and economic growth, total energy consumption in Australia has also increased accordingly. The government has invested more than US$5 billion in developing and commercialising clean energy technologies to reduce the nation's carbon footprint. The Department of Resources, Energy and Tourism is working with the Department of Climate Change and Energy Efficiency to develop an Energy Savings Initiative (ESI), a market-based tool for driving economy-wide improvements in energy efficiency (ABS, 2012; APERC, 2012; RET, 2012).

Energy industry: China

China is energy rich as a result of its huge coal reserves. Its huge population, growing economic base and energy consumption by heavy industry combine to make China the world's largest energy consumer. Despite the country looking to switching to cleaner fuel, the country's energy base remains dominated by coal. In 2008 China set up the National Energy Administration (NEA), a high-profile committee responsible for developing, implementing and administering energy industry planning as well as industrial policies and standards. Following recommendations from the committee, China is actively trying to secure its oil supply by investing abroad. The country is also inviting private capital participation and allocating the necessary resources to accelerate growth of the industry (APERC, 2012; BP, 2012).

Energy industry: Hong Kong

Hong Kong has no energy resources and has little choice but to import its energy. The two priorities of the government's energy policy are to ensure energy demands

Table 2.23 Energy industry in the GAPAC countries – key statistics

Country	Energy production (Mtoe)	Electricity consumption/population (MWh/capita)	CO_2 emissions (Mt of CO_2)	CO_2/GDP (kg CO_2/2005 USD)	Energy reserves (as of 2011)		
					Oil (billion barrels)	Gas (billion m³)	Coal (Mt)
Australia	296.73	10.51	396.77	0.44	4.1	2900	764000
Cambodia	3.79	0.17	4.03	0.43	0	0	7
China	2432.5	3.3	7954.55	1.9	14.784	2808	114500
Hong Kong	0.05	5.95	45.02	0.2	0	0	0
India	540.94	0.67	1745.06	1.32	5.8	1075	66800
Indonesia	394.57	0.68	425.88	1.06	4	3000	5500
Japan	51.67	7.85	1186.04	0.26	0.044	20900	350
Korea, South	46.99	10.16	587.73	0.56	0	3000	326
Malaysia	34.27	4.23	193.96	1.04	5.8	2500	1938
Myanmar (Burma)	22.39	0.12	8.25	0.45	na	na	na
New Zealand	-6.13	9.38	30.31	0.25	0.081	29.4	571
Philippines	23.89	0.65	77.12	0.57	0.1	70.4	0.449
Singapore	0.93	8.4	64.77	0.37	0	0	0
Sri Lanka	5.33	0.49	14.98	0.42	0	0	0
Taiwan	NA	NA	NA	NA	0.0028	6.2	1.1
Thailand	68.74	2.22	243.19	1.16	0.442	299.8	1239
Vietnam	65.6	1.07	137.36	1.75	615mt	600	6100

Source: IEA, 2011.

are met safely, efficiently and at reasonable prices and that energy is efficiently used and conserved. The country has targeted reducing energy use by 25 per cent (from the 2005 level) by 2030 (APERC, 2012).

Energy industry: India

A burgeoning population and massive economic growth have impacted India's energy consumption. A net importer of energy, India consumes roughly 3 per cent of the world's total energy, transported mostly via ship and pipeline. It has huge coal reserves and is the third largest coal-producing country in the world. India is looking to foreign investment to meet its huge energy demand. However, there need to be improvements in infrastructure and bureaucracy before this can be attracted (APERC, 2012; FEI, 2002).

Energy industry: Indonesia

The energy industry in Indonesia plays a major role in the economy. The country has huge oil, gas and coal reserves. Indonesia's 2007 Energy Law outlined its energy policies and regulations to ensure energy security and at the same time promote fair competition between enterprises in the energy supply chain (APERC, 2012).

Energy industry: Japan

Japan is one of the world's largest oil consumers. It imports most of its energy resources from the Middle East, Australia, Indonesia, Russia, China, Canada, the US and South Africa. The Ministry of Economy, Trade and Industry (METI) is responsible for regulating the industry, developing mineral resources, ensuring energy supply and promoting efficient use of energy. METI's key objectives are to achieve the 3Es: energy security, economic growth and environmental protection. Part of the 3E initiative involved fully replacing standard light bulbs with energy-saving lighting to improve energy efficiency (APERC, 2012; BP, 2012).

Energy industry: South Korea

Paradoxically, despite having no oil resources, South Korea is a key manufacturer in the global automobile industry. The country is home to many industries that depend on huge amounts of energy to operate: semiconductors, shipbuilding, petro-chemicals, digital electronics, steel, machinery, parts and materials. This dependence on imported energy made South Korea the world's fifth largest importer of oil and the world's second largest importer of coal and liquefied natural gas (LNG) in 2010. Despite the energy industry being mostly owned and governed by the government, in recent years the sector has been opened up to private investment. The government has put in place a long-term energy strategy for the industry to follow until 2030. The key goals include improving energy efficiency and reducing energy consumption, increasing the supply of clean energy and reducing the use of fossil fuels, boosting the green energy industry and ensuring citizens have access to affordable energy (APERC, 2012).

Energy industry: Malaysia

Malaysia has huge energy reserves and is a net energy exporter. Australia, Thailand, India, China, Japan and Korea are the main export destinations. The government's energy policy consists of three elements: (1) ensure an adequate, secure and cost-effective supply of energy; (2) promote efficient utilisation of energy and discourage wasteful and non-productive patterns of energy consumption; and (3) minimise the negative impacts of energy production, transportation, conversion, utilisation and consumption on the environment (APERC, 2012; DOS, 2011).

Energy industry: Myanmar (Burma)

To reach its target economic growth of 8 per cent per annum, Myanmar will need as much energy as it can produce. Geological surveys confirm the country has 7.8 trillion cubic feet of proven natural gas reserves, worth about US$75 billion. Though global energy companies have shown great interest in exploiting onshore and offshore fuel, a shortage of skilled HR and requisite expertise, corruption and lack of a proper regulatory framework are hindering progress (Farzad, 2013).

Energy industry: New Zealand

New Zealand has more than enough energy resources to meet domestic demand. The energy industry in New Zealand is co-regulated by the government and the Gas Industry Company, the industry body. Energy efficiency has always been a key goal of the industry. In 2011 the government announced the New Zealand Energy Efficiency and Conservation Strategy 2011−16 (NZEECS) which has the overall goal of improving the country's energy intensity (energy consumed per unit GDP) by 1.3 per cent per year until 2016 (APERC, 2012).

Energy industry: the Philippines

The primary objective of the energy industry in the Philippines is to achieve energy independence. In its 2012−2030 Philippine Energy Plan, the Department of Energy emphasised the importance of creating a future with less carbon. It also promoted investment in the energy industry and improving energy efficiency. The 'Bright Now! Do Right, Be Bright' campaign was launched by the government in 2011 to promote energy conservation. The six sectors it targeted were commercial and government buildings, industrial/manufacturing, residential, power, transport and agriculture. As part of the campaign, nine programmes were developed: (1) Social Mobilisation, Information, Education and Communication; (2) Energy Efficiency Standards and Labelling; (3) Government Energy Management; (4) Energy Management Services/Energy Audits; (5) Voluntary Agreement; (6) Recognition

Award; (7) Fuel Economy Run; (8) Locally Funded Projects that Promote Energy Efficiency and Conservation and (9) Foreign Assisted/Technical Assistance (APERC, 2012).

Energy industry: Singapore

Singapore has no natural resources and has little choice but to import its energy resources to meet domestic demand. In 2010 the government's Economic Strategies Committee (ESC) proposed a number of key strategies to meet its energy policy objectives: (1) diversify energy supplies; (2) enhance infrastructure and systems; (3) improve energy efficiency; (4) strengthen the green economy and (5) pricing energy right. The government has introduced many measures to encourage energy efficiency and ensure energy security, such as the Grant for Energy Efficiency Technologies (GREET) scheme (a co-funding scheme launched in 2008 to incentivise owners or operators of industrial facilities to invest in energy-efficient technologies or equipment), the Investment Allowance Tax Scheme (to encourage companies to invest in energy-efficient equipment) and the Singapore Certified Energy Manager (SCEM) training programme (to provide a thorough understanding of the key energy issues facing the building and energy industry sectors). These measures help participants develop the technical skills and competencies needed to manage the energy issues of the organisations they serve (APERC, 2012; ESC, 2010).

Energy industry: Sri Lanka

As a result of the huge demand for energy in Sri Lanka, the country's dependence on coal imports and spiralling energy costs, Sri Lanka is making efforts to generate renewable energy (i.e., solar energy, which it has in abundance) and to construct coal power plants. China and India are currently providing Sri Lanka with the necessary expertise to make its renewable energy capacity more cohesive. Rising energy demands coupled with lack of energy infrastructure and skilled HR are challenges that need to be addressed (Böck, 2012).

Energy industry: Taiwan

Taiwan has very few energy reserves and consequently imports most of its domestic energy requirements. The government encourages the use of renewable energy sources, including wind power, solar energy and biomass burning. Though not a signatory to the Kyoto Protocol, the government has promoted a reduction in carbon dioxide emissions and plans to impose restrictions on emissions from Taiwan's top-200 energy consumption enterprises (Clough, 2007).

Energy industry: Thailand

Despite having moderate energy reserves, Thailand imports large amounts of energy, particularly oil, to meet domestic demand. The energy industry is

influenced by five strategies put forward by the government: ensuring energy security; development of alternative energy; supervising energy prices and safety;
energy conservation and efficiency; and environmental protection. To ensure
national energy security, the government is planning to intensify energy development by conducting exploration and development of energy resources domestically
and internationally and by negotiating with neighbouring countries for the joint
development of energy resources (APERC, 2012; EDMC, 2012).

Energy industry: Vietnam

The energy industry in Vietnam is a major contributor to the economy. Despite
Vietnam having energy reserves and being a net energy exporter of crude oil and
coal, it is expected to become a net energy importer after 2015. In order to ensure
its energy security, the country will need to look again at its energy supply and
usage, devise adequate energy-efficient methods and develop the necessary infrastructure to meet increasing demand. Vietnam is looking to widen international
cooperation to strengthen its energy industry (APERC, 2012).

Summary

The energy industry plays a central role in economic development, but it is the
latter that determines the demand for energy. The energy industry is responsible for
harnessing natural reserves, finding innovative ways of increasing the efficient use
of energy and maintaining a balance in light of climate change. Though the
GAPAC is energy rich in terms of natural reserves, there is much to be done to
bring about innovative ways of improving energy efficiency.

Conclusion

This chapter outlines the specific issues and challenges facing tourism and hospitality, retail, healthcare, education, security and energy (including oil, gas and renewables) in the 17 economies of the region. Key statistics about our six focus
industries such as the total contribution of each industry to employment (number of
jobs generated directly in the industry plus indirect and induced contributions) and
GDP are presented. The chapter sets the stage for Chapter 3 in which we discuss
the efficiency of the labour market in these industries across the region.

Notes

1. NCEA stands for National Certificate of Educational Achievement.
2. Customary authority relates to that of indigenous peoples as opposed to international legal
   authority.

References

ABS. (2012). *Australian national accounts: National income, expenditure and product (Cat. No. 5206.0).* Canberra: Australian Bureau of Statistics.

ADB. (2005). *$1 million grant approved to support Philippine health sector reform.* Asian Development Bank. Available from <http://www.adb.org/news/1-million-grant-approved-support-philippine-health-sector-reform>.

AIC. (2010). *Australian crime: Facts and figures 2009.* Canberra: Australian Institute of Criminology.

APCCA. (1999). *World prison population stats.* Hong Kong: Asian and Pacific Conference of Correctional Administrators.

APERC. (2012). *APEC energy overview 2012.* Japan: Asia Pacific Energy Research Centre.

Austrade. (2013). *China's online retail sector: October 2013.* Sydney, Australia: Austrade.

Austrade. (2014). Singapore healthcare industry gaps offer numerous opportunities. Available from <https://www.austrade.gov.au/education/news/updates/singapore-healthcare-industry-gaps-offer-numerous-opportunities#.U0FSb97xuM8>.

Australian Government. (2009). *National energy security assessment 2009.* Canberra: Australian Government. Available from <www.ret.gov.au/energy/Documents/Energy%20Security/National-Energy-SecurityAssessment-2009.pdf> Accessed on 10.02.13.

Azar, K. (2013). *Trends of shopping malls and retail industry in Hong Kong.* Hong Kong: The French Chamber of Commerce & Industry. Available from <http://www.fccihk.com/files/dpt_image/4_events/eflyer/Event2013/131126_KarimAzar/French%20Chamber%20of%20Commerce_26%20Nov%202013.pdf> Accessed on 08.02.14.

B2B Cambodia. (n.d). *Safety, security & insurance.* B2B Cambodia. Available from <http://www.b2b-cambodia.com/b2b-safety-security/> Accessed on 14.03.13.

Bangkok Post. (2014). Thailand's consumer confidence at 26-month low. *Bangkok Post,* 10 February 2014.

Barcelona, N. (2010). Philippine health sector dying, says doctors' alliance. *CBCPNews.com.* Available from <http://pilipinasreporter.wordpress.com/2010/03/15/philippine-healthcare-system-dying%E2%80%94head/>.

BBC. (2014). *India visa-on-arrival scheme to be extended.* BBC. 6 February 2014. Available from <http://www.bbc.com/news/world-asia-india-26062351> Accessed 10.02.14.

BBC News. (2005). *South Korea's education success.* Seoul: BBC News. 13 September 2005. Available from <http://news.bbc.co.uk/go/pr/fr/-/2/hi/uk_news/education/4240668.stm>.

BBC News. (2011). *Changing Taiwan faces new challenges.* Taipei: BBC News. 30 September 2011. Available from <http://www.bbc.com/news/world-radio-and-tv-15064520> Accessed on 14.03.13.

Bellman, E. (2014). Indonesia launches universal healthcare. *Wall Street Journal,* 13 January 2014.

BICC. (2006). *Security sector reform in Indonesia.* BICC (Bonn International Center for Conversion). Available from <http://www.bicc.de/ssr_gtz/pdf/indonesia.pdf> Accessed on 14.03.13.

Böck, H. (2012). *Sun or coal? Sri Lanka's energy dilemma.* Deutsche Welle. 14 February 2012. Available from <http://www.dw.de/sun-or-coal-sri-lankas-energy-dilemma/a-15741574> Accessed on 10.02.13.

BP. (2012). *Statistical review of world energy 2012.* BP. Available from <www.bp.com/statisticalreview> Accessed on 10.02.13.

Brisbanetimes. (2014). Malaysia expects little tourism impact from missing flight MH370. *Sydney Morning Herald*, 17 March 2014. Available from <http://www.smh.com.au/travel/travel-incidents/malaysia-expects-little-tourism-impact-from-missing-flight-mh370-20140317-hvjki.html#ixzz2wBA7N1N9> Accessed 17.03.14.

Broadhurst, R.G. (2000). *Crime trends in Hong Kong: another look at the Safe City*. Paper presented at *Second Annual Conference of the Hong Kong Sociology Association, 25 November 2000, The Hong Kong University of Science and Technology*.

Button, M. (2006). The private security industry in South Korea: A familiar tale of growth, gaps and the need for better regulation. *Security Journal, 19*, 167–179.

Cambodia Herald. (2014). Cambodia boosts education reform. Available from <http://www.thecambodiaherald.com/cambodia/detail/1?page=15&token=OWNkNjQwZmU5MDA#sthash.XHP1gU9z.dpuf> Accessed 25.03.14.

Carvalho, M. (2013). Malaysia has potential to be regional healthcare hub, says Najib. *The Star Online*. Available from <http://www.thestar.com.my/News/Nation/2013/09/17/najib-tun-razak-healthcare-service-providers.aspx/> Accessed 04.02.14.

Chambers, P. (2014). *Obstacles to civilian control of the security sector in Thailand*. Thailand: Institute of Southeast Asian Affairs.

Chee, K. (2010). Call to overhaul of security industry. *my paper Singapore*, 21 October, 2010. Available from <http://news.asiaone.com/News/AsiaOne+News/Singapore/Story/A1Story20101021-243402.html> Accessed 12.02.14.

Chheang, V. (2008). The political economy of tourism in Cambodia. *The Asia Pacific Journal of Tourism Research, 13*(3), 282–297.

Chheang, V. (2009). *Tourism development in Cambodia: Opportunities for Japanese companies*. Tokyo: Japan External Trade Organization. Available from <http://www.ide.go.jp/English/Publish/Download/Brc/pdf/02_ch1.pdf> Accessed 06.01.14.

Chheang, V. (2013). *Cambodian security and defence policy*. Tokyo: The National Institute of Defense Studies. Available from <http://www.nids.go.jp/english/publication/joint_research/series9/pdf/01.pdf> Accessed 12.02.14.

CIA World Factbook. (2012). Education expenditures. *CIA World Factbook*. Available from <http://www.nationsencyclopedia.com/WorldStats/CIA-Education-expenditures.html> Accessed 10.02.14.

CII. (2014). *Healthcare sector*. Confederation of Indian Industry. Available from <http://www.cii.in/Sectors.aspx?enc=prvePUj2bdMtgTmvPwvisYH+5EnGjyGXO9hLECvTuNu2yMtqEr4D408mSsgiIyM/>.

Clark, N. (2013). *Vietnam: Trends in international and domestic education*. World Education News and Reviews. 1 June 2013. Available from <http://wenr.wes.org/2013/06/vietnam-trends-in-international-and-domestic-education/>.

Clough, L. D. (2007). Energy profile of Taiwan. *Encyclopedia of earth*. Available from <http://www.eoearth.org/view/article/152534>.

Contact Singapore. (2014). Healthcare services. Available from <http://www.contactsingapore.sg/key_industries/healthcare_services/>.

Cosgrove, C. (2008). Bill to overhaul New Zealand's security industry. behive.govt.nz. Available from <http://www.beehive.govt.nz/release/bill-overhaul-new-zealand%E2%80%99s-security-industry> Accessed 10.02.14.

CSPIA. (2012). *China security industry development report*. Beijing: China Security and Protection Industry Association.

Cunningham, G. (2011). *Gradually gaining traction: Overview of the Cambodian economy*. Phnom Penh: Cambodia Capital.

Curriculum Project. (n.d.). *Education in Burma and on the border.* Burma: Curriculum Project. Available from <http://curriculumproject.org/education-in-burma> Accessed on 27.01.13.

Deloitte. (2013a). *The Philippines: What's next for the chosen land?* London: Deloitte.

Deloitte. (2013b). *Reflections on education and technological development in China 2013.* London: Deloitte.

Department of Resources, Energy and Tourism (RET), (2012). Energy White Paper 2012. Department of Resources, Energy and Tourism, Australia. Available from <www.ret. gov.au/energy/facts/white_paper/Pages/energy_white_paper.aspx> Accessed 23.08.13.

Department of Statistics (DOS). (2011). *Petroleum and natural gas statistics 2011.* Department of Statistics, Malaysia. Available from <www.statistics.gov.my/portal/ index.php?option=com_content&view=article&id=1865%3Apetroleum-and-natural-gas-statistics&catid=42%3Apublications&lang=en> Accessed 08.02.14.

Department of Statistics Malaysia. (2012). *Domestic tourism survey 2011.* Department of Statistics, Malaysia. Available from <http://www.statistics.gov.my/portal/images/stories/ files/LatestReleases/findings/SUMMARY_FINDINGS_DTS2011.pdf> Accessed 16.03.14.

DFAT. (2011). *Analysis of Australia's education exports.* Canberra: Department of Foreign Affairs and Trade.

Digal, L. (2001). An analysis of the structure of the Philippine retail food industry. *Philippine Journal of Development, 51, XXVIII.* (No. 1) First Semester 2001.

DNA India. (2013). Ground zero summit 2013, Asia's largest information security conference, launched. *dnaindia.com*, 9 August 2013. Available from <http://www.dnaindia.com/ press-releases/press-release-ground-zero-summit-2013-asias-largest-information-security-conference-launched-1872304> Accessed 10.01.14.

DOS. (2014). *Retail sales index food & beverage services index December 2013.* Singapore: Department of Statistics.

DOTP. (2014). *DOT unveils new award to celebrate tourism excellence.* DOT Media Center, DOT Philippines. Available from <http://www.tourism.gov.ph/pages/default.aspx> Accessed 16.03.14.

Dyck, J., Andrea, E. W., & Fahwani, Y. R. (2012). *Indonesia's modern food retail sector: Interaction with changing food consumption and trade patterns (EIB-97).* Washington, DC: US Department of Agriculture, Economic Research Service.

EABFU. (2013). *2012 Economic Background and 2013 Prospects.* Hong Kong: Economic Analysis and Business Facilitation Unit.

EconomyWatch. (2010). Education sector. *EconomyWatch*, 29 June 2010. Available from <http://www.economywatch.com/world-industries/education-industry.html>.

EIU. (2013). *Cambodia's retail revolution?* Economist Intelligence Unit, 31 October 2013.

Energy Data and Modelling Center (EDMC). (2012). *APEC energy database.* Japan: Institute of Energy Economics. Available from <www.ieej.or.jp/egeda/database> Accessed 07.02.14.

ESC. (2010). *Report of the economic strategies committee: High skilled people, innovative economy, distinctive global city.* Singapore: Economic Strategies Committee.

Euromonitor (2013). World Retail Data and Statistics 2014. Available from <http://www. euromonitor.com/medialibrary/PDF/Book_WRDAS_2014.pdf> Accessed 07.02.14.

Express TravelWorld. (2014). *India and Japan in MoU to strengthen tourism sector.* Express TravelWorld, 26 February 2014. Available from <http://travel.financialexpress.com/ latest-updates/2258-india-and-japan-ink-mou-to-strengthen-tourism-sector>.

Farzad, R. (2013). *The rush to tap Myanmar's energy promise.* Bloomberg Businessweek, 07 June 2013 Available from <http://www.businessweek.com/articles/2013-06-07/the-rush-to-tap-myanmars-energy-promise> Accessed 07.02.14.

FBIC. (2013). *Retail market in China September 2013*. Hong Kong: Fung Business Intelligence Centre.

Fennell, D. (1999). *Ecotourism: An introduction*. London: Routledge.

FICCI. (2013). *Private security industry in India*. New Delhi: Federation of Indian Chambers of Commerce and Industry.

Flath, D., & Nairu, T. (1992). *Is Japan's retail sector truly distinctive?* Working paper no. 72. New York: Center on Japanese Economy and Business, Columbia University.

Fossil Energy International (FEI). (2002). An energy overview of India. Available from <http://www.geni.org/globalenergy/library/national_energy_grid/india/energy_overview_of_india.shtml> Accessed 09.02.14.

GBG. (2012). *Education in Indonesia: Overview*. Global Business Guide. Available from <http://www.gbgindonesia.com/en/education/article/2011/education_in_indonesia_overview.php>.

GBG. (2013). *Indonesia's tourism industry and the creative economy*. Global Business Guide. Available from <http://www.gbgindonesia.com/en/services/article/2012/indonesia_s_tourism_industry_and_the_creative_economy.php>.

Ghosh, P. (2013). Vietnam: A police state where one-in-six works for security forces. *International Business Times*, 29 August 2013 Available from <http://www.ibtimes.com/vietnam-police-state-where-one-six-works-security-forces-1401629> Accessed 12.02.14.

GLD. (2010). *The six industries where Hong Kong enjoys clear advantages: Progress in brief*. Hong Kong: Government Logistics Department, Hong Kong Special Administrative Region Government.

GSV. (2012). *Education sector: Factbook 2012*. Chicago, IL: Global Silicon Valley.

Hall, S. T., & Lewis, M. (2008). *Education in China: 21st century issues and challenges*. Hauppauge, NY: Nova Science Publishers.

Harish, R. (2014). *Will visa power boost India's tourism?* East Asia Forum. Available from <http://www.eastasiaforum.org/2014/03/07/will-visa-power-boost-indias-tourism/> Accessed 10.02.14.

Harper, D. (2007). Energy, online etymology dictionary. Available from <http://www.etymonline.com/index.php?term=energy> Accessed 18.02.14.

Havocscope. (2014). Ranking of illegal economic activities. Available from <http://www.havocscope.com/country-profile/> Accessed 12.03.14.

Henke, N., & Kadonaga, S. (2009). *Improving Japan's health care system*. London: McKinsey.

HKTB. (2013). *Hong Kong: The facts (tourism)*. Hong Kong: Hong Kong Tourism Board.

IBEF. (2013). *Indian tourism and hospitality industry: An overview*. India Brand Equity Foundation. Available from <http://www.ibef.org/industry/tourism-and-hospitality-snapshot> Accessed 06.01.14.

IE Singapore. (2013). *The Singapore advantage*. Singapore: International Enterprise.

IEA. (2011). *Country indicators for 2011*. Intelligence Energy Agency. Available from <http://www.iea.org/statistics/statisticssearch/report/?&country=AUSTRALI&year=2011&product=Indicators>.

IM. (2012). *Myanmar retail: An unseen opportunity?* Invest in Myanmar, 7 December 2012.

Interpol (n.d). Singapore police force. *Interpol*. Available from <http://www.interpol.int/Member-countries/Asia-South-Pacific/Singapore> Accessed 12.02.14.

Invest in Australia (2013). Education and training industry in Australia. Available from <http://investinaustralia.com/current-opportunities>.

ISDS. (2011). *Developing a security sector reform index (SSRI) in the Philippines: Towards conflict prevention and peace building*. Institute for Strategic and Development Studies.

Available from <http://www.isdsphilippines.org/index_files/projects.htm> Accessed 30.01.14.

JETRO. (2007). *Japanese trade and investment statistics*. Japan External Trade Organisation. Available from <http://www.jetro.go.jp/en/stats/statistics/bpfdi_01_e.xls> Accessed 10.07.12.

Jing, L., & Ghosh, S. (2009). Protection and enforcement of well-known mark rights in China: History, theory and future. *Northwestern Journal of Technology and Intellectual Property*. Available from <http://scholarlycommons.law.northwestern.edu/njtip/vol7/iss2/1>.

JNTO. (2013). *Latest topics*. Japan National Tourism Organization. Available from <http://www.jnto.go.jp/eng/topics/2013/president_message_20131220.html> Accessed 06.01.14.

Ken Research. (2012). Japan education industry forecast to 2015. Available from <http://www.marketresearch.com/Ken-Research-v3771/Japan-Education-Forecast-7158295/>.

Ken Research. (2013). South Korea's education industry lies amongst the highly developed and most competitive industries in the world. A high academic orientation has henceforth promoted the growth of the pre-primary sector since very long. StudyMode.com. Available from <http://www.studymode.com/essays/South-Korea%E2%80%99s-Education-Industry-Lies-Amongst-1930101.html> Accessed 21.01.14.

Kittikanya, C. (2005). Thailand: Private security booms with insecurity. *Bangkok Post*, 18 April 2005.

KTO. (n.d.). *Visitor arrivals, Korean departures, international tourism receipts and expenditures*. Korea Tourism Organization. Available from <http://english.visitkorea.or.kr/enu/index.kto> Accessed 26.01.14.

Kurniawan, H. (2014). Indonesian retail sector sees more growth. *Jakarta Globe*, 17 February 2014. Available from <http://www.thejakartaglobe.com/business/indonesian-retail-sector-sees-more-growth/>.

lankanewspapers.com (2006). Private security in Sri Lanka. lankanewspapers.com, 6 June 2006. Available from <http://www.lankanewspapers.com/news/2006/6/7206.html> Accessed 18.02.14.

Loh, L. (2010). It's no longer 'Uniquely Singapore' but 'Your Singapore' now. CNN, 8 March 2010. Available from <http://travel.cnn.com/singapore/play/signapore-tourism-board-your-singapore-rebranding-campaign-388837>.

Loke, D. (2011). *Business environment of education industry in Malaysia, August 2011 class of international MBA*. Zurich, Switzerland: University of Applied Sciences.

MBIE. (2013). *The New Zealand sectors report 2013: Tourism*. Wellington: Ministry of Business Innovation and Employment, New Zealand Government.

MED. (2013). *Medical tourism in 2013, facts and statistics*. Medical Tourism Resource Guide. Available from <http://www.medicaltourismresourceguide.com/medical-tourism-in-2013>.

Ministry of Education Republic of China (2013). *Education in Taiwan*. Ministry of Education Republic of China (Taiwan).

Mishkin, S. (2012). Chinese tourists boost Taiwan economy. *Financial Times*, 30 August 2012. Available from <http://www.ft.com/cms/s/0/b231cf10-f248-11e1-8973-00144feabdc0.html#axzz2xhA9v21j>.

MOE-NZ. (2009). *The New Zealand education system: An overview*. Ministry of Education New Zealand. Available from <http://www.minedu.govt.nz/~/media/MinEdu/Files/EducationSectors/InternationalEducation/ForInternationalStudentsAndParents/NZEdSysOverview.pdf>.

MOE-S. (2013). Singapore, raising the bar on quality. Speech by Senior Minister of State, Ms Indranee Rajah at *Private Education Conference 2013, 9 April 2013*.

MOE-T. (2008). *Towards a learning society in Thailand: An introduction to education in Thailand*. Ministry of Education Thailand. Available from <http://www.bic.moe.go.th/th/images/stories/book/ed-eng-series/intro-ed08.pdf>.

MOFAT. (2013). *Taiwan tourism bureau launches the Taiwan giveaways app campaign*. Ministry of Foreign Affairs. Available from <http://www.taiwanembassy.org/US/SFO/ct.asp?xItem=457890&ctNode=3015&mp=67>.

MOHM. (2010). *Economic transformation programme: A roadmap for Malaysia*. Ministry of Health Malaysia. Available from etp.pemandu.gov.my/...National_Key_Economic_Areas-@-Healthcare.aspx.

MOHT. (2013). *Myanmar, Tourism Master Plan 2013–2020 (Final Draft Report, June)*. Yangon, Myanmar: Ministry of Hotels and Tourism.

MOTM. (2013). Malaysia country report. Paper presented at CAP-CSA and UNWTO conference on sustainable tourism development, 12–14 April 2013, Hyderabad, India [Ministry of Tourism Malaysia].

MTANZ. (n.d.). *Overview*. Auckland, New Zealand: Medical Technology Association of New Zealand.

Muncaster, P. (2013). Japan needs 80,000 EXTRA info-security bods to stay safe. *The Register*, 9 October 2013. Available from <http://www.theregister.co.uk/2013/10/09/japan_infosecurity_skills_shortage/> Accessed 15.02.14.

Naidu, R. (2013). Gangnam Style brings fans, tourism to South Korea. CNBC, 24 January 2013. Available from <http://www.globalpost.com/dispatch/news/regions/asia-pacific/south-korea/130124/gangnam-style-Psy-korea-tourism>.

Niyogi, S. (2013). *South Korea in hot pursuit of Indians*. Kolkata: TTG Asia Media, 12 March 2013. Available from <http://www.ttgmice.com/article/south-korea-in-hot-pursuit-of-indians/>.

NZRA. (2013). *The retail market in New Zealand: An analysis*. Wellington: New Zealand Retailers Association.

NZSA. (n.d.). *The security industry*. New Zealand Security Association. Available from <http://security.org.nz/dev/about-nzsa/the-security-industry/> Accessed 10.02.14.

NZT&E. (2007). *Japan 2007: Education market profile*. Hamilton, New Zealand: New Zealand Trade & Enterprise.

OECD. (2013). *Economic outlook for South East Asia, China and India 2014: Beyond the middle income trap*. Organisation for Economic Co-operation and Development. Available from <http://www.oecd.org/site/seao/Cambodia.pdf> Accessed 10.02.14.

Pavey, E., & Smith, C. (2009). Post-conflict reconstruction and security sector reform in Sri Lanka. In H. Born, & A. Schnabel (Eds.), *Security sector reform in challenging environments* (pp. 189–210). Münster, Germany: Lit Verlag.

PC. (2011). *Overview: Economic structure and performance of the Australian retail industry*. Canberra: Productivity Commission.

People's Daily (2001). China makes progress in adopting new technology in education. Available from <http://english.peopledaily.com.cn/english/200108/21/eng20010821_77924.html>.

Phys.org (2012). Japan security firm to offer private drone. Phys.org, 27 December 2012. Available from <http://phys.org/news/2012-12-japan-firm-private-drone.html> Accessed 26.01.14.

PI. (2011). *Private security contractors outnumber police 2 to 1 worldwide*. Public Intelligence, 13 July 2011. Available from <http://publicintelligence.net/private-security-contractors-outnumber-police-2-to-1-worldwide/> Accessed 10.01.14.

PME Jobs Network. (2012). *Retail industry*. Singapore: PME Jobs Network.

Prenzler, T., Earle, K., & Sarre, T. (2009). Private security in Australia: Trends and key characteristics. *Trends and issues in crime and criminology, 374*, 1−6.

Prosser, K. (2013). *Hong Kong's healthcare market: Lessons from the budget*. Hong Kong: EC Harris Asia Pacific.

PTI. (2013). *India's healthcare sector to grow to $158.2bn in 2017*. New Delhi: Press Trust of India.

PwC. (2011). *2012 Outlook for the retail and consumer products sector in Asia*. London: PricewaterhouseCoopers.

PwC. (2012). *Checking up on Taiwan healthcare: Market challenges and opportunities*. Taipei, Taiwan: PricewaterhouseCoopers.

Radio Australia. (2014). China's booming outbound tourism industry. ABC, 20 January 2014. Available from <http://www.radioaustralia.net.au/international/radio/program/asia-pacific/chinas-booming-outbound-tourism-industry/1250554> Accessed 26.01.14.

RAM. (2012). *Sri Lanka economic outlook 2013*. Kualalumpur: RAM Holdings Berhad.

RAM. (2013). *Private pills for public pains*. Colombo: Lanka Rating Agency.

Ramos, M. (2009). PNP to require specialized training for private security guards. *Philippine Daily Inquirer*, 21 October 2009. Available from <http://newsinfo.inquirer.net/breaking-news/nation/view/20091021-231509/PNP-to-require-specialized-training-for-private-security-guards> Accessed 12.02.14.

ReportLinker (2014). Healthcare industry: Market research reports, statistics and analysis. Available from <http://www.reportlinker.com/ci02241/Healthcare.html>.

Rivers, W. P. (1998). Is being there enough? The effects of homestay placements on language gain during study abroad. *Foreign Language Annals, 31*(4), 492−500.

Rodas, A. (2012). The boom of the Cambodian tourist industry. Tourism Cambodia. Available from <http://www.tourismcambodia.org/news/index.php?view=detail&nw=96> Accessed 18.02.14.

Rungfapaisarn, K. (2013). Retail growth expected on economic stimulus. *The Nation*, 31 January 2013. Available from <http://www.nationmultimedia.com/business/Retail-growth-expected-on-economic-stimulus-30199046.html>.

SAL. (2008). *Study of Hong Kong's industry level competitiveness: The tourism sector*. Hong Kong: Strategic Access Limited.

Samedi. (1997). *Security firms see robust market*. Taiwan Info. Available from <http://taiwaninfo.nat.gov.tw/ct.asp?xItem=15597&CtNode=103&htx_TRCategory=&mp=4> Accessed 10.02.14.

Sanjeed, V. K. (2009). Vietnam healthcare: The next growth frontier? *Asia Pacific Biotech News, 13*(10), 18. <www.asiabiotech.com >.

Shah, A. (2011). Health care around the world. Global Issues, 22 September 2011. Available from <http://www.globalissues.org/article/774/health-care-around-the-world> Accessed 12.02.14.

Sheng, L., & Zhao, J. (2010). Understanding China's retail market. *China Business Review*, 1 May 2010.

Shobert, B. (2013). Healthcare in Myanmar. Forbes.com, 19 August 2013. Available from <http://www.forbes.com/sites/benjaminshobert/2013/08/19/healthcare-in-myanmar/>.

SIPRI. (2012). *SIPRI military expenditure database*. Stockholm International Peace Research Institute. Available from <http://milexdata.sipri.org> Accessed 10.02.14.

Song, K. (2009). Major problems in Korean security industry. *Korea IT Times*, 24 November 2009. Available from <http://www.koreaittimes.com/story/5887/major-problems-korean-security-industry> Accessed 10.02.14.

STB. (2013). Navigating the next phase of tourism growth. Paper presented at *Tourism Industry Conference 2013, Singapore* [Singapore Tourism Board].

Sternquist, B., & Jin, B. (1998). South Korean retail industry: Government's role in retail liberalization. *International Journal of Retail & Distribution Management, 26*(9), 345–353.

Sukma, R. (2013). *Indonesia's security outlook, defence policy and regional cooperation.* Japan: The National Institute for Defense Studies. Available from <http://www.nids.go.jp/english/publication/joint_research/series5/pdf/5-1.pdf> Accessed 10.02.14.

Sun Ten (n.d.). SUN TEN receives superior tourism factory award from Taiwan Ministry of economic affairs. Sun Ten. Available from <http://www.suntenglobal.com/news/show.php?ID=116>.

Tang, S. M. (2011). Malaysia's security outlook and challenges. *Asia Pacific countries' security outlook and its implications for the defense sector* (NIDS Joint Research Series 6). Tokyo: National Institute for Defense Studies.

TDN. (2014). Thailand records historical high in tourist arrivals in 2013. *Travel Daily News,* 15 January 2014. Available from <http://www.traveldailynews.asia/news/article/54539/thailand-records-historical-high-in>.

Thayer, C. (2012). *Vietnam's security outlook.* Tokyo: The National Institute for Defense Studies (NIDS).

The Business Times. (2013). Tourists spent more than USD2.6b on shopping in Malaysia in 2012. *The Business Times,* 19 November 2013. Available from <http://www.retailinasia.com/category/markets/malaysia> Accessed 16.02.14.

The Economist. (2011a). The world in figures: Industries – health care. The Economist, 17 November 2011. Available from <http://www.economist.com/node/21537945> Accessed 08.01.14.

The Economist. (2011b). Education in South Korea glutted with graduates. *The Economist,* 3 November 2011. Available from <http://www.economist.com/blogs/banyan/2011/11/education-south-korea#sthash.NbPNgGy7.dpuf>.

The Malaysian Insider. (2012). 11,000 Nepalese work as security guards in Malaysia. *The Malaysian Insider,* 9 October 2012. Available from <http://www.themalaysianinsider.com/malaysia/article/11000-nepalese-work-as-security-guards-in-malaysia> Accessed 14.02.14.

The Star Online. (2014). Malaysia's retail sector saw sluggish 3.1% Q3 sales growth. *The Star Online,* 16 January 2014. Available from <http://www.thestar.com.my/Business/Business-News/2014/01/16/Sluggish-Q3-sales-growth-Retail-sector-saw-31-sales-growth-with-tighter-debt-control/> Accessed 16.02.14.

Thwe, E. (2013). *Retail distribution in frontier market.* Yangon, Myanmar: Beauty Palace Co. Ltd. (Cute Press).

Timetric Research. (2013). Japan's tourism industry to recover after tsunami and nuclear crisis. Available from <https://timetric.com/info/media-center/press-releases/2013/05/13/japans-tourism-industry-recover-after-tsunami-and-nuclear-crisis/> Accessed 08.01.14.

TITC. (2013). *Positive signs for Viet Nam tourism in the first 6 months.* Tourism Information Technology Center. Available from <http://vietnamtourism.gov.vn/english/index.php/items/6043>.

Tourism Australia. (2011). *Tourism 2020.* Canberra: Australian Government, Department of Resources, Energy and Tourism.

Toyabe, S. (2009). Trend in geographic distribution of physicians in Japan. *International Journal for Equity in Health 2009, 8,* 5. Available from <http://www.equityhealthj.com/content/8/1/5>.

UKTI. (2013). *Education sector in Indonesia*. UK Trade & Investment. Available from <http://opentoexport.com/article/education-sector-in-indonesia-2/>.

UN. (2012). *Security sector reform (SSR) perspective*. New York: United Nations. Available from <https://www.un.org/en/events/peacekeepersday/pdf/securityreform.pdf> Accessed 12.02.14.

UNESCO. (2009). *Facing global and local challenges: the new dynamics for higher education — Sri Lanka country report*. UNESCO. Available from <http://portal.unesco.org/geography/fr/files/10905/12353682765Sri_Lanka.pdf/Sri%2BLanka.pdf>.

UNICEF. (2011). *Education sector*. UNICEF. Available from <www.unicef.org/cambodia>.

USDA/FAS. (2013). *Vietnam retail foods: Sector report 2013, Hanoi, Vietnam*. Washington, DC: US Department of Agriculture/Foreign Agricultural Service.

USDOC. (2011). *Doing business in Cambodia: Country commercial guide for U.S. companies*. US Department of Commerce.

Walsh, C. (2012). *The healthcare market in South Korea*. PMGroup Worldwide. Available from <http://www.pmlive.com/pharma_intelligence/country_report_the_healthcare_market_in_south_korea_404120#contents>.

WDA. (2012). *Factsheet on security industry and security Singapore: Workforce skills qualifications*. Singapore: Workforce Development Agency.

Webber, A. (2010). *Literature review: Cost of crime*. Parramatta, Australia: Attorney General and Justice.

WEF. (2013). *The travel & tourism competitiveness index 2013*. World Economic Forum. Available from <http://www3.weforum.org/docs/TTCR/2013/TTCR_CountryHighlights_2013.pdf>.

Wharton School. (2007). *China's healthcare industry is hot, and investors are paying attention*. Wharton School of the University of Pennsylvania. Available from <http://www.knowledgeatwharton.com.cn/index.cfm?fa=viewArticle&articleID=1747>.

Wikipedia. (2012). Health care system in Japan. Available from <http://en.wikipedia.org/wiki/Health_in_Japan> Accessed 26.01.14.

Wikipedia. (2013a). Individual visit scheme. Available from <http://en.wikipedia.org/wiki/Individual_Visit_Scheme> Accessed 26.01.14.

Wikipedia. (2013b). Health care industry. Available from <http://en.wikipedia.org/wiki/Health_care_industry> Accessed 26.01.14.

Wikipedia. (2014). List of countries by number of police officers. Available from <http://en.wikipedia.org/wiki/List_of_countries_by_number_of_police_officers> Accessed 26.01.14.

Wonderful Indonesia. (2013). *Indonesia tourism performance 2012*. Jakarta, Indonesia: Ministry of Tourism and Creative Economy.

World Bank. (2006). *Education in Vietnam history, challenges and solutions*. World Bank. Available from <http://siteresources.worldbank.org/EDUCATION/Resources/278200-1121703274255/1439264-1153425508901/Education_Vietnam_Development.pdf>.

World Bank. (2011). *Thailand: challenges and options for 2011 and beyond*. World Bank. Available from <http://www-wds.worldbank.org/external/default/WDSContentServer/WDSP/IB/2012/03/20/000333038_20120320230302/Rendered/PDF/674850Revised00y0Note0master0110901.pdf>.

World Bank. (2012). *Military expenditure (% of central government expenditure)*. World Bank. Available from <http://data.worldbank.org/indicator/MS.MIL.XPND.ZS/countries> Accessed 10.02.14.

World Bank. (2013a). *Cambodia: Education sector*. World Bank. Available from <http://go.worldbank.org/Y1ZC3ETHR0> Accessed 10.02.14.

World Bank. (2013b). *Sri Lanka: Helping children get and finish a better education*. World Bank. Available from <http://go.worldbank.org/Y6CUVBBU11>.

World Bank. (2013c). *World development indicators*. Washington, DC: World Bank.

Worldwatch Institute. (2013). China to become second largest tourism economy within the decade. Available from <http://www.worldwatch.org/node/3920> Accessed 26.01.14.

WTO. (1993). *Tourism development and the responsibility of the State*. Madrid: World Tourism Organization.

WTO. (2013). *Tourism highlights 2013 edition*. Madrid: World Tourism Organization.

WTTC. (2012). *Japan's tourism economy to stage full recovery in 2012*. World Travel and Tourism Council. Available from <http://www.wttc.org/news-media/news-archive/2012/japans-tourism-economy-stage-full-recovery-2012/>.

WTTC. (2014a). *Economic data search tool*. London: World Travel and Tourism Council.

WTTC. (2014b). *South Korea's Travel & Tourism sector set to outperform economy over next ten years*. World Travel and Tourism Council. Available from <http://92.52.122.233/news-media/news-archive/2014/south-koreas-travel-tourism-sector-set-outperform-economy-over-n/>.

WTTC. (2014c). *Travel & tourism: economic impact 2013 − Hong Kong*. London: World Travel and Tourism Council.

Xinhua. (2013). Taiwan to open tourism to more mainland. *Xinhua*, 16 June 2013. Available from <http://www.chinadaily.com.cn/china/2013-06/16/content_16627776.htm>.

Yoshida, N., & Leishman, F. (2006). Plural policing in Japan. In T. Jones, & T. Newburn (Eds.), *Plural policing in comparative perspective*. London: Routledge.

Changing HR landscapes across the region

3

Introduction

In Chapters 1 and 2 we discussed the significance of the greater Asia Pacific (GAPAC) region. We now know that the region is a paradox in that it is the world's growth engine, on the one hand, yet it is one of the most poverty-stricken and environmental disaster-prone zones of the world, on the other. It is also home to labour-intensive economies, rising domestic demand for quality goods and services as well as economies relying heavily on exports. The region is gradually shifting from agricultural and manufacturing-based economies to more knowledge-driven service-oriented economies. Hence, in the coming years it is the knowledge base that will drive labour market efficiency.

Labour market efficiency in a knowledge-based economy and the role HR plays

A labour market can broadly be defined as a system in which work is exchanged for capital (Fay, 2011). Driven by supply and demand, the labour market is primarily one of two types: internal or external. The internal labour market relates to the specific characteristics that exist within an organisation such as its business/HR policies, practices and priorities and its stock of HR. The external labour market relates to the external supply or labour available outside the organisation and is affected not only by the business/HR policies, practices and priorities of the organization, but also by multiple factors like industry-specific skills demand, changing demography, and government regulations (Wilton, 2010).

The World Economic Forum (WEF) explains labour market efficiency as, 'the efficiency and flexibility of the labour market are critical for ensuring that workers are allocated to their most efficient use in the economy and provided with incentives to give their best effort in their jobs. Labour markets must therefore have the flexibility to shift workers from one economic activity to another rapidly and at low cost, and to allow for wage fluctuations without much social disruption. The importance of the latter has been dramatically highlighted by the recent events in Arab countries, where high youth unemployment sparked social unrest in Tunisia that spread across the region. Efficient labour markets must also ensure a clear relationship between worker incentives and their efforts to promote meritocracy at the workplace, and they must provide equity in the business environment between women and men. Taken together these factors have a positive effect on worker performance and the attractiveness of the country for talent, two aspects that are growing more important as talent shortages loom on the horizon' (WEF, 2013, pp. 6–7).

The World Economic Forum (WEF) measures the following ten parameters to arrive at overall scores for labour market efficiency:

   i. *Cooperation in labour–employer relations.* Lower scores in this parameter mean relations are generally confrontational whereas higher scores mean relations are generally cooperative.

   ii. *Flexibility of wage determination.* This measures whether wages are generally set by a centralised bargaining process or by each individual company.

   iii. *Hiring and firing practices.* This parameter looks at whether such practices are heavily impeded by regulations or whether they are extremely flexible.

   iv. *Redundancy costs.* These costs are measured in terms of weeks of salary.

   v. *Effect of taxation on incentives to work.* This measures the extent to which taxes reduce the incentive to work.

   vi. *Pay and productivity.* This measures the extent to which pay is related to labour productivity.

   vii. *Reliance on professional management.* This determines whether senior management positions are held by relatives or friends without regard to merit or whether they are held by professional managers chosen on merit and qualifications.

   viii. *Country capacity to retain talent.* This measures whether the best and brightest leave to pursue opportunities in other countries or whether they stay and pursue opportunities in the country.

   ix. *Country capacity to attract talent.* This measures whether the country attracts talented people from abroad or not.

   x. *Female participation in the labour force.* This measures the degree to which females participate in the workforce.

The knowledge economy is reshaping the labour market (Rowley & Poon, 2011). Such an economy rests on four pillars (World Bank Group, 2003, p. 2):

- A supportive economic and institutional regime that provides incentives for the efficient use of existing and new knowledge and the flourishing of entrepreneurship.
- An educated and skilled population to create, share and use knowledge.
- A dynamic information infrastructure to facilitate the effective communication, dissemination and processing of information.
- An efficient innovation system of firms, research centers, universities, consultants and other organisations that taps into the growing stock of global knowledge, assimilates and adapts it to local needs and creates new technology.

Thus, education, whether it be formal (structured programmes recognised by the formal education system), informal (structured programmes not formally recognised by the national system) or non-formal (unstructured learning taking place at home, in the community or workplace), plays an important role in maintaining the competitiveness of the country as well as of industries and individuals (World Bank

Group, 2003). Life-long learning has become important and acquiring new skills a necessity to survival in a knowledge-based economy and, consequently, such learning helps in building human capital, increasing economic growth and development and improving labour market efficiency.

Tables 3.1–3.3 show the global rankings of the GAPAC countries in 2013 and 2008 regarding labour market efficiency. Singapore improved its overall global rank from second to first. It is regarded as promoting meritocracy at the workplace, providing equity between women and men in the business environment and, consequently, attracting talent to its shores.

An overall look at the labour market efficiency scores shows Indonesia, Thailand, Australia and South Korea have experienced the sharpest fall in labour market efficiency (as indicated in Table 3.3). Hiring and firing practices, pay and productivity, cooperation in labour–employer relations and female participation are the key factors behind such a negative change in the situation – factors that are integral to the HR profession.

Therefore, it may be argued that HR policies, practices and priorities – be they at the organisational or country level – are at the core of the labour market and play a significant role. Labour market efficiency is about balancing the demand for labour with supply. Such a process includes matching available knowledge, skills and abilities to the work requirements of the organisation or country in order to convert work into capital. Interestingly, in a recent report the WEF identified skills mismatch as a serious issue affecting labour market efficiency where large-scale unemployment and talent scarcity go hand in hand (WEF, 2014). The report further highlights that HR practices – particularly, inefficient recruitment strategies – are a reason for such a mismatch. Cappelli (2012) also identified inadequate HR practices as having led to the imposition of exacting hiring criteria and hence to skills mismatch.

Clearly, for the region to remain the growth engine of the world, it has to improve its labour market efficiency and become knowledge driven, where education and life-long learning will be the key components driving competitiveness and success not only for organisations but also for economies. Human resources have a pivotal role to play in not only helping solve the skills mismatch issue but also in formulating a people strategy (Rowley & Jackson, 2011; Ulrich, 2012) for an efficient labour market. This will only be possible if they have the requisite credibilities/competencies. According to Ulrich (2012). they are Credible Activist, Capability Builder, Technology Proponent, Change Champion, HR Innovator & Integrator and Strategic Positioner. From the 'Reliance on professional management' scores in Tables 3.1 and 3.2, we gained an overview into whether senior management roles are held by relatives or friends without regard to merit or whether professional managers are chosen on merit and qualifications. Yet, owing to the ever-increasing significance of HR professionals in improving the economy of a country, industry or organisation, it is important to see who might take the HR profession to the next level.

Table 3.1 Labour market efficiency global ranks – 2013

Country	Cooperation in labour–employer relations	Flexibility of wage determination	Hiring and firing practices	Redundancy costs (in weeks of salary)	Effect of taxation on incentives to work	Pay and productivity	Reliance on professional management	Country capacity to retain talent	Country capacity to attract talent	Female participation in labour force	Overall global rank of labour market efficiency
Australia	103	135	137	49	59	113	11	37	17	60	54
Cambodia	68	71	15	93	30	32	78	44	51	16	27
China	60	94	28	120	42	17	44	31	26	36	34
Hong Kong	8	4	1	17	5	1	28	7	5	85	3
India	61	50	52	76	67	58	46	50	54	137	99
Indonesia	49	106	39	141	27	29	34	39	28	115	103
Japan	9	11	134	9	76	13	17	29	80	90	23
Korea, South	132	61	108	120	111	21	43	25	31	97	78
Malaysia	19	33	26	110	10	2	21	20	22	121	25
Myanmar (Burma)	131	23	41	NA	73	89	141	148	122	20	98
New Zealand	11	10	61	1	13	16	1	79	29	49	8
Philippines	34	109	117	124	40	44	32	71	86	111	100
Singapore	2	5	3	6	4	4	8	8	2	84	1
Sri Lanka	53	65	132	142	55	39	33	103	117	132	135
Taiwan	25	31	55	105	77	6	23	48	59	87	33
Thailand	37	111	31	135	44	31	57	27	32	65	62
Vietnam	64	69	81	111	99	15	119	95	69	21	56

Source: WEF (2013).

Table 3.2 Labour market efficiency global ranks – 2008

Country	Cooperation in labour-employer relations	Flexibility of wage determination	Non-wage labour costs	Rigidity of employment)	Hiring and firing practices	Firing costs*	Pay and productivity	Reliance on professional management	Brain drain	Female participation in labour force	Overall global rank of labour market efficiency
Australia	37	75	85	4	46	7	26	4	38	42	9
Cambodia	113	84	1	90	47	70	64	121	55	6	33
China	65	52	126	32	53	108	9	46	36	32	51
Hong Kong	7	1	18	1	7	91	1	27	12	60	4
India	44	54	69	48	104	85	45	24	49	122	89
Indonesia	19	79	30	87	19	117	18	47	19	102	43
Japan	6	14	46	18	111	7	12	17	14	79	11
Korea, South	95	43	46	65	45	108	14	42	33	80	41
Malaysia	13	42	60	14	42	95	6	22	29	107	19
Myanmar (Burma)	NA	NA	NA	NA	NA	NA	NA	NA	NA	NA	NA
New Zealand	32	29	9	8	103	1	25	2	91	30	10
Philippines	71	108	24	61	101	108	57	40	116	86	101
Singapore	2	4	46	1	2	7	2	8	13	83	2
Sri Lanka	76	76	60	40	75	123	53	43	54	116	115
Taiwan	12	12	46	104	25	108	4	35	27	72	21
Thailand	17	91	20	21	39	84	43	59	31	38	13
Vietnam	91	101	69	40	40	103	17	95	88	10	47

*Firing costs (in weeks of wages) - This variable estimates the cost of advance notice requirements, severance payments, and penalties due when terminating a redundant worker, expressed in weekly wages.
Source: WEF (2008); The World Bank. *Doing Business 2008.*

Table 3.3 Labour market efficiency comparison

Country	Labour market efficiency (2013)			Labour market efficiency (2008)			Net change in overall rank of labour market efficiency
	Over all score	Global rank	Rank among the 17 focus countries of the greater APAC region	Over all score	Global rank	Rank among the 17 focus countries of the greater APAC region	
Australia	4.5	54	9	5.1	9	3	−45
Cambodia	4.8	27	6	4.7	33	9	6
China	4.6	34	8	4.5	51	13	17
Hong Kong	5.7	3	2	5.6	4	2	1
India	4.1	99	14	4.2	89	14	−10
Indonesia	4	103	16	4.6	43	11	−60
Japan	4.8	23	4	5.1	11	5	−12
Korea, South	4.2	78	12	4.6	41	10	−37
Malaysia	4.8	25	5	4.9	19	7	−6
Myanmar (Burma)	4.1	98	13	NA	NA	NA	NA
New Zealand	5.2	8	3	5.1	10	4	2
Philippines	4.1	100	15	4.1	101	15	1
Singapore	5.8	1	1	5.7	2	1	1
Sri Lanka	3.5	135	17	3.9	115	16	−20
Taiwan	4.7	33	7	4.8	21	8	−12
Thailand	4.3	62	11	5	13	6	−49
Vietnam	4.4	56	10	4.5	47	12	−9

Source: WEF (2008, 2013).

Like it or loathe it: HR landscapes are changing across the region

Aei4eiA[1] examined the social media profiles of senior HR professionals from across the region to get a feel for the profession. It randomly sampled 170 LinkedIn (LI) profiles (10 from each of our 17 focus countries). LI is a business-oriented social networking site for professionals; its slogan is 'relationships matter' (LinkedIn, 2014). Boyd and Ellison (2007) define social network sites as web-based services that allow individuals to construct a public or semi-public profile within a bounded system, articulate a list of other users with whom they share a connection and view and traverse their list of connections and those made by others within the system. Despite having its own limitations regarding the validity of the information, the study carried out by Aei4eiA provides a broad overview of the existing state of the HR profession.

Through LI's 'Advanced People Search' option, we typed 'HR' in the 'Key Words' box, selected 'Country' (inputting our 17 focus countries one at a time), and finally searched '3rd + Everyone Else' with at least '10 years of experience'. In this way we allowed for the selection of random profiles. Every tenth profile was selected for coding. As a result of limited resources, we used ten profiles per country (i.e., a total of 170 profiles) for the purpose of analysis. The profile page was the unit of analysis. We recorded the following variables: country, gender, organisation type (multinational company, MNC; large local firms; small and medium enterprises, SMEs; not-for-profit organisations, NFPs), educational qualifications, working experience (in years), total connections on LI, LI recommendations received, skills endorsements received from connections. The designations for our people search ranged from Senior HR Director, HR Director, General Manager, Chief HR, HR Leader, National HR Manager, Group Head HR, Senior Vice President-HR, HR Business Partner (HRBP) to HR Manager.

What we found was interesting at the macro level. Of our total of 170 samples of senior HR professionals, 50 per cent were male and 50 per cent female. Over 60 per cent had BSc degrees (in HR or a related subject) whereas only 50 per cent had MSc or higher degrees (in HR or related subjects). Nearly 70 per cent were very well connected, with 400+ LI connections, but 60 per cent did not receive any recommendations for their professional work from their connections, despite the skills of over 90 per cent being endorsed. Nearly one third (32 per cent) had fewer than 15 years of experience, over one third (37 per cent) had between 15 and 20 years of experience and over one quarter (28 per cent) over 20 years. The details are presented in Table 3.4.

By comparing country-specific characteristics with these labour market efficiency ranks, we were able to derive relevant information on the 17 GAPAC countries in our study (see the following subsections).

Australia (n = 10)

Despite an overall decline in female participation in Australia's labour force, female HR professionals dominate. Fewer than 5 have a BSc degree in HR or related

Table 3.4 Summary of the LinkedIn profile analysis of senior HR professionals across the GAPAC region

Gender (*n* = 170)	
M	**F**
85 (50%)	85 (50%)
Received skills endorsements from connections	
Yes	**No**
158	12
Total number of LI connections	**Percentage**
500+ 400+ 300+ 200+ 100+ Less than 100	61 9 12 10 5 3
Educational qualifications	**Percentage (*n* = 170)**
Bachelors *(in HR or related subject)* Masters or higher degree *(in HR or related subject)* Masters *(in other subject)* Any certificate *(in HR or related subject)*	66 58 2 37
Years of experience (in years)	**Total percentage**
10 to15 15 to 20 >20 Did not mention	32 37 28 3
LI recommendations received	**Percentage**
0 1 to 5 6 to 10 More than 10	63 26 8 3

Note: Descriptive statistics from 170 publicly available LinkedIn profiles of senior HR professionals compiled by Aei4eiA in 2014.

subject, 5 have a skills enhancement Certificate in HR or related subject and just 2 have a MSc or higher degree in HR or related subject. The majority (8) have at least 15 years experience and are well connected (with 500+ connections). Even though hiring and firing was identified as a key sub-factor in the sharpest decline in rank (from 46 in 2008 to 137 in 2013), each received skills endorsements from connections and 6 received at least one recommendation, including 3 having received 10 or more.

Cambodia (n = 10)

Despite a decline in female participation in Cambodia's labour force, the country improved its rank in all other factors of labour market efficiency. This was also reflected in our study of 6 male professionals. All have at least a BSc degree in HR or related subject, the majority (9) have a certificate in HR or related subject as well and 7 have a MSc or higher degree in HR or related subject. The majority (8) have 10−15 years of experience and 7 are well connected (with 500+ connections). Most (9) received skills endorsements from connections, but only one received at least one recommendation.

China (n = 10)

Over the years China has struggled to maintain flexibility in wage determination, but its hiring and firing practices have improved. Despite a slight decline in female participation in the labour force, there are just as many male and female HR professionals. Six professionals have a BSc in non-HR subjects and a MSc or higher degree in HR or related subject. China's ranking in 'Reliance on professional management' has improved. This is reflected in our study where the majority (7) have at least 15 years of experience and 8 are well connected (with 400+ connections). All received skills endorsements from connections, but only one received a recommendation.

Hong Kong (n = 10)

There has been a steep decline in female participation in Hong Kong's labour force. Six of our 10 HR professionals were male. Of the 10 professionals in our study, 6 have a BSc in HR or related subject and the majority (7) have a MSc or higher degree in HR or related subject as well. Five have more than 10 but less than 15 years of experience. The remaining 5 have more than 15 years of experience and are well connected, with the majority (6) having 400+ connections and the rest at least 200+ connections. All received skills endorsements from connections but only 4 received recommendations from their connections.

India (n = 10)

Despite a decline in India's ranking in 'Reliance on professional management', hiring and firing practices in the country have progressed. Of the 10 professionals in our study, 7 were male HR professionals. Of our 10 professionals, 7 have a BSc in HR or related subject, all have a MSc or higher degree in HR or related subject and a majority (8) have a skill enhancement certificate in HR or related subject as well. Seven have more than 15 years of experience and are well connected (with 500+ connections). All 10 received skills endorsements from connections and 9 received recommendations from their connections, with one receiving over 40 recommendations.

Indonesia (n = 10)

Other than Indonesia's ranking in 'Reliance on professional management', its ranking in all other parameters of labour market efficiency declined. Indonesia is one of three countries in the region whose ranking in overall labour market efficiency experienced the sharpest decline. Female participation in the labour force has declined. Indeed, 8 of the HR professionals in our study were male. Of the 10 professionals, 7 have a BSc in HR or related subject, only 4 have a MSc or higher degree in HR or related subject and none has a skill enhancement certificate in HR or related subject. Seven have more than 15 years of experience and 8 are well connected (with 500+ connections). All received skills endorsements from connections and 6 received at least one recommendation from their connections.

Japan (n = 10)

Despite Japan increasing its ranking in 'Flexibility of wage determination' and maintaining its ranking in 'Reliance on professional management', hiring and firing practices and decline in female participation in the labour force have been identified as factors negatively affecting labour productivity. Of the 10 professionals in our study, 7 were male. Of our 10 professionals, 9 have a BSc in HR or related subject, only 2 have a MSc or higher degree in HR or related subject and none has any skill enhancement certificate in HR or related subject. All have more than 15 years of experience and are moderately connected. Five have 400+ connections. Seven received skills endorsements from connections but only one received a recommendation from connections.

Korea, South (n = 10)

South Korea's ranking in labour market efficiency rank fell dramatically. An equal number of male and female HR professionals were recorded in our study. Eight have a BSc in non-HR subjects, 5 have a MSc or higher degree in HR or related subject and none has any skill enhancement certificate in HR or related subject. Of the 10 professionals in our study, 9 have more than 15 years of experience and are moderately connected. Of our 10 professionals, 4 have 500+ and 6 at least 200+ connections. Eight received skills endorsements from connections but only 2 received a recommendation from connections.

Malaysia (n = 10)

Malaysia improved its 'Pay and productivity' ranking and the country's hiring and firing practices also recorded growth. Despite the number of females in the workforce falling, 6 HR professionals were female. Of the 10 professionals in our study, 7 have a BSc in HR and a related subject, 6 have a MSc or higher degree in HR or related subject and only 2 have a skill enhancement certificate in HR or related subject. Of our 10 professionals, 7 have more than 15 years of experience and are well connected. Seven have 400+ connections. Nine received skills endorsements from connections but only 3 received a recommendation from connections.

Myanmar (Burma) (n = 10)

In the absence of 2008 labour market efficiency data, we used currently available data for our analysis. According to 2013 statistics, Myanmar ranks 20 in the world in the number of females in the workforce and is one of the highest in the region. However, equal numbers of male and female HR professionals were noted in our study. Of the 10 professionals in our study, 6 have a BSc in HR and a related subject, 8 have a MSc or higher degree in HR or related subject and 6 have a skill enhancement certificate in HR or related subject. Five have less than 15 years of experience and are well connected. Seven have 500+ connections. All received skills endorsements from connections but only one received a recommendation from connections.

New Zealand (n = 10)

In 2013 New Zealand was globally ranked No. 1 for 'Reliance on professional management'. Interestingly, apart from its ranking declining in 'Female participation in labour force', the country scored well in all other parameters of labour market efficiency. The HR profession in New Zealand is female dominated. Of the 10 professionals in our study, 6 have a BSc in HR and a related subject, just 3 have a MSc or higher degree in HR or related subject and 6 have a skill enhancement certificate in HR or related subject. Eight have more than 15 years of experience (6 of whom with more than 20 years) and are moderately connected. Five have 400+ connections. They all received skills endorsements from connections but only one received a recommendation from connections.

The Philippines (n = 10)

The Philippines had a positive net change in its ranking for overall labour market efficiency. Improvements have been recorded in 'Co-operation in labour–employer relations' and 'Pay and productivity'. Despite a fall in the country's 'Female partic- ipation in labour force' ranking, the HR profession has bucked the trend by having many female professionals. Of the 10 professionals in our study, 8 have a BSc in HR and a related subject, 4 have a MSc or higher degree in HR or related subject and 4 have a skill enhancement certificate in HR or related subject. Seven have more than 15 years of experience and are well connected. Eight have 400+ connec- tions. They all received skills endorsements from connections and 5 received a recommendation from connections.

Singapore (n = 10)

Singapore has maintained its global leadership and is still ranked No. 1 for labour market efficiency despite its 'Pay and productivity' scores decreasing slightly over the years. An equal number of male and female HR professionals were found in our analysis. Of the 10 professionals in our study, 9 have a BSc in HR and a related subject, 7 have a MSc or higher degree in HR or related subject and 5 have a skill enhancement certificate in HR or related subject. Nine have more than 15 years of experience (5 of whom with more than 20 years) and are well connected. Seven have 500+ connections. All received skills endorsements from connections and 3 received a recommendation from connections.

Sri Lanka (n = 10)

Though similar to many countries in the region, Sri Lanka's overall labour market efficiency scores are low. The country has remarkably improved its 'Cooperation in labour–employer relations', 'Flexibility of wage determination', 'Pay and productivity' and 'Reliance on professional management' scores. Hiring and firing practices and the number of females in the workforce are responsible for the low scores. However, we found more female (6) than male HR professionals in our analysis. Of the 10 professionals in our study, 8 have a BSc in HR and a related subject, 9 have a MSc or higher degree in HR or related subject and 8 have a skill enhancement certificate in HR or related subject. Seven have less than 15 years of experience and are well connected. Seven have 500+ connections. All received skills endorsements from connections and 5 received a recommendation from connections.

Taiwan (n = 10)

Once known for its labour market efficiency, Taiwan's rankings declined with the notable exception of 'Reliance on professional management'. More female (6) than male HR professionals were recorded in our analysis. Of the 10 professionals in our study, 8 have a BSc in HR and a related subject, all have a MSc or higher degree in HR or related subject and 3 have a skill enhancement certificate in HR or related subject. Six have fewer than 15 years of experience and are well connected. Six have 500+ connections. All received skills endorsements from connections and 5 received a recommendation from connections.

Thailand (n = 10)

Thailand recorded a sharp decline in its ranking for labour efficiency measures. We found more male (8) than female HR professionals. Of the 10 professionals in our study, 7 have a BSc in HR and a related subject, 6 have a MSc or higher degree in HR or related subject and 4 have a skill enhancement certificate in HR or related subject. Eight have more than 15 years of experience and are well connected. Six have 450+ connections. All received skills endorsements and 5 received a recommendation from connections.

Vietnam (n = 10)

Hiring and firing practices, reliance on professional management and the number of females in the workforce are the three critical areas that are responsible for pulling down Vietnam's overall labour market efficiency scores. We found more female (8) than male HR professionals in our analysis. Of the 10 professionals in our study, 6 have a BSc in HR and a related subject, only 3 have a MSc or higher degree in HR or related subject and 3 have a skill enhancement certificate in HR or related subject. Five have fewer than 15 years of experience and are well connected. Nine have 500+ connections. Seven received skills endorsements from connections but only 3 received a recommendation from connections.

Conclusion

This chapter looks at the labour market efficiencies of our 17 focus countries. Interestingly, despite the GAPAC steadily growing in terms of increased business potential and consequent dynamism, the labour market efficiency of most of the countries is on the decline. This clearly shows that sustainable development of the region depends on the role played by human resources. However, are HR professionals skilled enough to be game changers? By examining the social media profiles of senior HR professionals we hope to have given some insight into this question.

Clearly, more work needs to be done. Human resources not only has to change to improve business bottom lines but has to do so much more quickly to cope with the changing business environment of the region. Chapter 4 presents ten case studies with a view to examining how organisations are dealing with challenges facing not only their businesses but also their human resources.

Note

1. Aei4eiA is a Sydney-based management, policy research and consultancy firm that focusses on people and sustainability matters.

References

Boyd, D. M., & Ellison, N. B. (2007). Social network sites: Definition, history, and scholarship. *Journal of Computer-Mediated Communication, 13*(1), 210–230, Blackwell.
Cappelli, P. (2012). *Why good people can't get jobs: The skills gap and what companies can do about it.* Philadelphia, PA: Wharton Digital Press.

Fay, C. (2011). Labour market. In C. Rowley, & K. Jackson (Eds.), *Human resource management: The key concepts* (pp. 122−127). London: Routledge.

Rowley, C., & Jackson, K. (2011). Introduction: HRM in context. In C. Rowley, & K. Jackson (Eds.), *Human resource management: The key concepts* (pp. xix−xxvii). London: Routledge.

Rowley, C., & Poon, I. (2011). Knowledge management. In C. Rowley, & K. Jackson (Eds.), *Human resource management: The key concepts* (pp. 118−122). London: Routledge.

Ulrich, D. (2012). *Human resource competency study 2012*. Provo, UT: RBL Group USA.

WEF. (2008). *The global competitiveness report 2008−2009*. World Economic Forum.

WEF. (2013). *The global competitiveness report 2013−2014*. World Economic Forum. Available from: <http://www3.weforum.org/docs/WEF_GlobalCompetitiveness Report_2013-14.pdf> Accessed 15.02.14.

WEF. (2014). *Matching skills and labour market needs building social partnerships for better skills and better jobs*. World Economic Forum. Available from: <http://www.weforum. org/reports/matching-skills-and-labour-market-needs-building-social-partnerships-better-skills-and-bette> Accessed 15.02.14.

Wilton, N. (2010). *An introduction to human resource management*. Thousand Oaks, CA: Sage Publications.

World Bank Group. (2003). Lifelong learning in the global knowledge economy: challenges for developing countries. Available from <http://siteresources.worldbank.org/INTLL/ Resources/Lifelong-Learning-in-the-Global-Knowledge-Economy/chapter1.pdf> Accessed 15.02.14.

Best HR practices: Insider view

4

Introduction

In Chapters 1–3 we documented how dynamisms in the greater Asia Pacific (GAPAC) are increasing and looked at some of the paradoxes and business and HR challenges that specific industries are facing. In this chapter we look at ten organisations belonging to our focus industries and operating in the region. We asked the interviewees (all senior representatives of the organisations) a set of questions:

- What are the top-three HR and business challenges facing their industry today?
- How prepared is their industry's HR to deal with such challenges?
- Can HR be a game changer and play a leading role in solving such challenges and help sustain businesses within their respective industry and, if so, how?
- What are the key HR risks facing their industry today and how can they be minimised?
- What specific HR best practices has their organisation put in place to withstand these HR/ business challenges?
- Given the ever increasing significance of technology in HRM, are their HR adequately equipped with the necessary technology competencies?
- What green initiatives (if any) have been taken by their organisation to deal with these HR and business challenges?
- To what extent are there linkages between their industry and other focus industries?
- What role does HR in their organisation play in harnessing the benefits of intra-industry and/or inter-industry linkages?
- Their opinion on the industry-specific challenges listed in Chapter 3.

Tourism and hospitality industry

As pointed out in Chapter 2, the tourism and hospitality sector is key to the economic growth of a country. The views of Eddie Lee, a senior HR professional at a major international airways company operating in Singapore, are pertinent. Eddie says,

> Asia is now regarded as the cash cow for growth. Businesses have evolved at a very fast pace whereas internal processes take time to catch up with the speed of growth. We need to hire a lot of people from the market to cope with the business growth. We have a dilemma whether to fill the positions with foreign talent or build local expertise. One thing most organisations fail to recognise is the potential of interns. Often interns are regarded as cheap labour and are not given enough attention. They are often given basic admin jobs. I think in order to cope with talent

shortages we need to brand organisation through internship scholarship while building a talent pipeline. I think HR can be a game changer. HR must organise a lot of forums and engage in communicating company policies with the employees while gathering feedback from the ground. Many a time, HR is reactive and often resort to firefighting. HR must be proactive. One of the key challenges that HR face is gaining a seat on the board especially in the APAC region where many HR activities are driven by the HQ.

Our first three case studies – India Tourism (Sydney), Singgasana Hotels and Resorts (Indonesia) and Grand Hotel (New Delhi) – give an insight into how multiple strategies and practices are being adopted at the organisation and the country level to promote growth in the industry.

Case Study 4.1 India Tourism (Sydney): 'Cheerfully Welcoming All to Incredible India!'

The Ministry of Tourism (MoT, Government of India) is the nodal agency formulating national policies and programmes for the development and promotion of tourism in India. The ministry has 20 field offices within the country and 14 overseas offices in Australia (Sydney), Canada (Toronto), China (Beijing), France (Paris), Germany (Frankfurt), Italy (Milan), Japan (Tokyo), the Netherlands (Amsterdam), Singapore, South Africa (Johannesburg), United Arab Emirates (Dubai), the UK (London) and the US (Los Angeles and New York). Like other overseas offices spread around the world, the key responsibilities of the Sydney office are to position India in the tourism-generating market as a preferred tourism destination, to promote various India tourism products and to increase India's share of the global tourism market (MoT, 2013a, p. 54). The Sydney office's jurisdiction covers Australia, New Zealand, Fiji, Pacific and the ASEAN[1] region. It is a mammoth task and the Sydney office is actively involved in 'Cheerfully Welcoming All to Incredible India!'.

Tourism in India (both domestic and international) is a huge industry turning over US\$121 billion and employing over 39 million people (WTTC, 2012). India is a melting pot of people and cultures, religions, food, geographic variations and much more. It is often described as a country with diametrically opposite elements from snow-clad mountains to scorching desert; one of the oldest civilizations of the world; a country with a rich heritage and home to the world's first planned cities, architectural splendour and infrastructural chaos; a country that is home to some of the world's best scientists, technocrats and entrepreneurs and to the largest number of semi-skilled adults in the world – a country that mesmerises all who visit it. With all its contrasting hues and wonders, the country is among the most interesting of destinations to visit. The year-on-year increase in the number of foreign tourists in India (estimated in 2012 to be 6.65 million), 851 million domestic tourists (estimated in 2011) and record foreign exchange earnings (FEEs) of INR94,484 crore (Indian rupees) in 2012 is testimony to the exponential growth of the industry (MoT, 2013a).

The vision of the MoT is to improve the quality of life of Indians by developing and promoting tourism, which would provide an opportunity for physical invigoration,[2] mental rejuvenation,[3] cultural enrichment and spiritual elevation (MoT, 2012a, p. 2). The MoT has a number of missions: (i) achieving a target of 10 million foreign tourist arrivals by 2016; (ii) achieving a target of 1450 million domestic tourist visits by 2016; (iii) positioning and maintaining tourism development as a national priority activity; (iv) enhancing and maintaining the competitiveness of the tourism industry; (v) improving existing tourism products and expanding them to meet new market requirements; (vi) creation of a world-class infrastructure; (vii) improving the visibility and attraction of the tourism sector to expand the potential of the market; (viii) augmenting the HR base; (ix) integrated development of major tourist destinations/circuits[4]; (x) promoting sustainable tourism (MoT, 2012a, p. 2).

'The Ministry has set a goal to increase India's share in the global tourism market. There is a strong focus on infrastructure development, development of niche products and manpower capability building. These we believe hold the key to India's sustained growth in the tourism sector,' says Madhu Dubey, Regional Director, India Tourism, Sydney.

The MoT has been making efforts to develop a tourism infrastructure at tourist destinations and circuits that is the envy of the region. At the beginning of each financial year, the MoT holds prioritisation meetings with each state/union territory (UT) to prioritise projects. Emphasis is given to selecting projects such as the construction and upkeep of wayside amenities along the highways/roads leading to tourist destinations, cleanliness at tourism sites as well as projects in backward areas (MoT, 2013a, p. 13). To promote India as a 365-day destination, to attract tourists with specific interests and to ensure repeat visits for the unique products in which India has comparative advantage, the MoT has also taken steps to identify, diversify, develop and promote niche products such as (a) cruises; (b) adventure holidays; (c) medical tourism; (d) wellness; (e) golf; (f) polo; (g) meetings, incentives, conferences and exhibitions (MICE); (h) ecotourism and (i) film tourism (MoT, 2013a, p. 19). Yet, how prepared is the industry's HR to deal with such enormous growth?

'In India it's all about numbers. Along with our focus on the international market, we have an enormous domestic market to cater to. In our industry, there is an immediate need to bridge the gap between demand and supply of skilled workforce. Over the years, more and more educated youths are entering the industry – which is a good sign. However, high employee turnover is a major concern for the industry. We have launched quite a few initiatives to tackle such challenges, notably through schemes like Hunar-Se-Rozgar Tak, Earn While You Learn, National Skill Testing and Certification Programme, *etc.,' explains Madhu.*

Hunar-Se-Rozgar Tak (meaning 'from skills to employment') was launched in 2009—10 not only to train 18 to 28-year-olds belonging to the economically weaker strata of society but also to give them the necessary employable skills. Its basic objectives are to reduce the skills gap in the hospitality and tourism sector and to ensure the economic benefit of tourism spreads to the poor. The programme offers a broad range of short-duration courses of six to eight weeks in areas like food and beverage services, food production, housekeeping and other training areas to improve the performance of stakeholders like drivers, golf caddies, security guards and tourist facilitators.[5] 'Earn While You Learn' is a 21-day training programme to inculcate in HR the appropriate tourism travel traits and knowledge for them to work as student volunteers. College-going students pursuing graduation courses or graduates in the 18—25 age group are eligible for the programme. The National Skill Testing and Certification Programme, on the other hand, has been devised to test and certify the skills of existing service providers (MoT, 2012b, p. 1).

In addition to the above, the MoT actively promotes and conducts capacity-building programmes for its employees. Intended to enhance the cross-functional competencies of employees the MoT has designed courses for their employees that include a variety of topics ranging from policy formulation and international tourism trends to computer application and communication skills. The MoT also recognises that women play a pivotal role in the industry and stresses the need for gender sensitisation and ensuring equal rights. Women officials from the MoT predominate at the headquarters, regional offices and overseas offices (MoT, 2013b, p. 89).

The MoT's list of actionable agendas for the next five years includes: (1) Tourist Facilitation & Security Organization (TFSO) pilot schemes to be launched in selected states/UTs of India in collaboration with the Ministry of Defence (Directorate of Re-Settlement) and their extension to other states/UTs; (2) adoption of Code of Conduct of Safe & Honourable Tourism guidelines for the approval of service providers and hotels; (3) introduce a new category of specialist guides comprising scholars (holding doctorates in Indian history, architecture and culture) and proven experts; (4) introduce a programme of refresher courses for licensed guides and (5) work with the Ministry of Civil Aviation/airline sector to improve the connectivity of important destinations to international and domestic markets (MoT, n.d., p. 11).

Realizing the potential of tourism as a driver of economic growth and development, the MoT launched the 'Incredible India' international marketing campaign in 2002. This very successful campaign was aimed at building the brand image of the country in global markets and at increasing foreign tourist arrivals and foreign exchange earnings (ICMR, 2006). This was complemented in 2008 by the *Atithi Devo Bhava* campaign (Wikipedia, 2013). Derived from a Sanskrit verse meaning 'Guest is God', it narrates an ancient Hindu scripture which became part of Hindu society etiquette on the relationship between a host and a guest. It was targeted at the local population to inform them of the economic benefits of tourism and to reiterate the spirit of the age-old belief that 'Guest is God'. Another recent initiative by the MoT is its 'Clean India' campaign. Launched in 2012, the campaign has the objective of addressing issues regarding cleanliness in and around tourist destinations. Following its launch, the MoT signed a memorandum of understanding (MOU) with the Ministry of Railways to work together towards a sustained sensitisation campaign[6] for train travellers and service providers under the Capacity Building for Service Providers scheme of the MoT and towards consultations and discussions with stakeholders, including the travel trade, to develop strategies for the upkeep and cleanliness of stations and coaches (PIB, 2012).

'We regularly co-ordinate with our stakeholders to address various issues such as steps to substantially reduce the gap in the availability of skilled manpower in the hospitality sector, to create necessary educational and training infrastructure, to facilitate improvement in the quality of the existing tourism infrastructure and encourage the creation of a new infrastructure, to promote sustainable tourism in the country and develop niche tourism products. We are striving for sustainable tourism by encouraging stakeholders to adopt eco-friendly practices. To encourage stakeholders achieve excellence in their areas of operation and promote good practices in the industry, we have also instituted Annual National Awards,' explains Madhu.

The MoT annually presents National Tourism Awards to various segments of the travel, tourism and hospitality industry. These awards are presented to state governments/UTs, classified hotels, heritage hotels, approved travel agents, tour operators and tourist transport operators, individuals and private organisations in recognition of their outstanding performance in their respective fields as well as to encourage healthy competition with the aim of promoting quality tourism. In keeping with the changing tourism scenario, the ministry introduced a number of new categories of awards in 2011–12: Best Medical Tourism Facilities; Best Tour Operator Promoting Niche Segments; Best State: Campaign Clean India; Best Heritage City; Best Heritage Walk; and Best Tourism Film (PIB, 2013).

When asked about her observations on the situation of Indian tourism in Australia, Madhu says:

Having been in this market for more than a year now I have observed two unique features. (a) This is a market that is interested in India primarily for culture, adventure and wellness tourism. And (b) broadly there are two segments of Australian travellers visiting India: (i) young travellers with mid to low budgets are mostly interested in adventure activities and exotic experiences and (ii) mature travellers with high-spending ability are interested in culture, wellness and luxury products. Interestingly, most of them come back with a happy experience to share and a good number of them are repeat visitors inclined to explore newer tourist destinations in their subsequent visits to India.

India has become the tenth most visited destination by Australians who make 214,000 visits a year (2012), up from 4000 in 2002 (Martin, 2012). Much of this is down to the initiatives, well-thought-through strategies and hard work of the MoT. The Sydney office recently won the Best Stand over 36 m^2 Award at the prestigious

Asia-Pacific Incentives and Meetings Expo 2013 held in Melbourne, where it was recognised for creating a welcoming and eye-catching display that captured the essence of the country and its products (AIME, 2013). When congratulated on receiving the award, Madhu enthusiastically said:

> *It's good to know that even good news spreads. We are a government body determined to meet our objectives in creating greater awareness about India in this region. We deal with business challenges like economic recession, connectivity issues, infrastructure and other concerns both for international as well as domestic tourists. It is our endeavour to promote India as an amazing multi-product year-round destination.*

Case Study 4.2 Singgasana Hotels and Resorts: 'a Majestic Presence with a Promise of Superior Services'

Singgasana is a Sanskrit word meaning 'lion's seat'. It is synonymous with the throne of a ruler, the seat of power from which ceremonial functions are conducted. Singgasana Hotels and Resorts is a hospitality management company with deluxe and first-class hotels, residences, golf courses and international convention centres in key destinations in Indonesia (namely, Jakarta, Bali, Surabaya, Makassar and Lombok). The hotel architecture is majestic and takes on the aura of a throne. Against such a backdrop, the hotel group promises to provide its guests with genuinely warm Indonesian hospitality (Singgasana Hotels and Resorts, 2013).

> *'In our organisation, HR plays a major role by working as a catalyst to help build strategies. We help implement strong professional development and review (PDR) with a focus on leadership competencies, skill sets and KPIs [key performance indicators], which is linked to a pay system and development system. We set strategies based on a KPI balanced scorecard,' says Wayan Carma, Director HR and Finance, Singgasana Hotels and Resorts, Indonesia.*

Recent years have seen increases in the number of hotels, to cater for rising numbers of tourists. The challenge for the hotel chain is to maintain service quality. Singgasana Hotels and Resorts boasts that all their services reflect the unique essence of Indonesian culture and heritage. However, Wayan is mindful of the people challenges that affect overall business:

> *The two key challenges are to retain the best talent in this competitive hotel industry and to maintain the productivity level of employees. High labour cost and low productivity are key people-related risks. In order to minimise such risks we believe in implementing a good recruiting, employee relation and reward system.*

As a result of rapid economic growth in the tourism sector, Singgasana Hotels and Resorts is constantly looking out for opportunities to manage and develop new properties in the future, and in so doing provide its signature Indonesian hospitality services and quality. The group aims to provide premium world-class hospitality services whilst investing in HR and facilities to maximise long-term stakeholder value.

Case Study 4.3 Grand Hotel (New Delhi): 'Providing Comfort to Customers'

The Grand New Delhi is a well-known 5-star hotel in Delhi. Set in 10 acres of grounds, the hotel blends modern design with contemporary comfort. With 30,000 ft^2 of meeting and banquet space, the hotel's Grand Ballroom is one of the largest pillarless banqueting facilities in the city. Known for its high levels of service excellence, the Grand is a much-sought-after destination for all kinds of events. Despite the huge growth in the tourism and hospitality industry in India, as a result of high competition and tourists who are spoilt for choice, the overall occupancy level has decreased (Talreja, 2013; The Grand, 2013).

> *'In the hospitality industry in India talent attraction and engagement are the biggest challenges. Industry has grown manifold since with the fast-paced growth there are multiple opportunities available and the expectations of employees have increased to an unjustified level. And HR has to keep looking for reasons and ways to keep employees engaged while keeping costs down due to budget constraints,' says Deepak Behl, Director of Human Resources, The Grand New Delhi.*

Deepak is a former Deputy Superintendent of Police who served in nine states of India, where he took on many challenging postings. He joined the hospitality industry over a decade ago. The training he received as a police officer, which principally involved safety and security issues, set him in good stead for his HR role, which back then in India mainly dealt with poor industrial relations, trade unionism, collective bargaining and labour–management relations.

> *With rising security concerns in the tourism and hospitality industry, I find my previous experiences as a cop to be a boon.*

Furthermore, the Grand recently invited a senior Army professional to give its female employees training in self-defence.

Professionals from the tourism and hospitality industry in India admit that talent attraction, retention and engagement are the key HR challenges facing their business.

> Today, in our industry competition has increased manifold. Many new hotels including international brands with the best available training and development facilities have set up shop. In order to maintain our service standards we have to ensure that we are providing the best of facilities to keep customers happy, employees engaged and costs in check. Instead of sending employees for training, experts from different fields are being invited to share their insights with the employees and their spouses. It is a good motivational exercise.

Retail industry

As pointed out in Chapters 1–3, the retail industry is diverse and covers a wide range of products and services. Rapid growth, fast-changing consumer behaviour, decreasing profitability, rising HR costs and intense competition are the order of the day. Our next three case studies – OfficeWorks (Australia), Unilever (Sri Lanka) and Nokia (India) – are good examples of this.

Case study 4.4 Officeworks: 'Big ideas. Lowest Prices'

Officeworks is Australia's leading retailer and supplier of office products and solutions for home, business and education. Founded in 1994 and later acquired by the Australian conglomerate Wesfarmers in 2007, it now has more than 140 stores, a strong online presence, over 15,000 products and in excess of 6000 employees across Australia. In 2012, Officeworks underwent a major rebranding, adding a human element to its cost-focussed advertising. Its new slogan 'Big Ideas. Lowest Prices' emphasises the role it plays in the daily lives of Australians (Officeworks, 2012).

> 'We recognised that we needed a better way to connect with our customers in a two-way dialogue, and subsequently a new creative approach was developed. Officeworks' role as one of Australia's leading retailers goes far beyond providing products and services – we are a part of something bigger. We play a role in the hopes and dreams of Australians – we are part of every office, every school bag and every business start-up, so it just made sense to tell these stories. Our new tagline embodies this – it's about communicating how Officeworks helps customers achieve more in their lives, while making sure they don't pay any more than they need to,' states Officeworks Managing Director Mark Ward.

Officeworks' colourful, bright and active Facebook page now has over 28,000 fans and has established itself as an active forum to engage with customers and

other stakeholders. The six business principles the company takes pride in are excellence, recognition, innovation, collaboration, communication and integrity. Moreover, the company gives its employees three guarantees: (1) a challenging and enjoyable work environment; (2) an opportunity to develop new skills with great training and development programmes; and (3) a chance to take an active role in driving the business forward.

'We value our employees and their hard work is always rewarded. Our team members get a variety of learning opportunities and initiatives. We make them aware of the business challenges. Retail study tours are organised and selected team members travel to countries like the United States and the United Kingdom to study best practices in retailing. For instance, in the early years we took our learnings from Home Depot and Disney from a cultural perspective. Officeworks' team members enjoy access to a great range of opportunities and discounts on things like private health insurance, health and fitness, travel, accommodation and more. They also have the opportunity to participate in the Wesfarmers Employee Share Offer where share options are allocated annually to enable them to share in the business's success. So they have a vested interest in the organisation,' explains Martin Duffy, General Manager Human Resources at Officeworks.

As the company is continually growing, it is fully aware of the HR and business challenges it faces:

'There are four key challenges we face today. (i) Diversity — our workforce is a diverse one. Therefore, we constantly strive to maintain a consistent and inclusive organisational culture and find answers to diversity-related challenges like how to address intergenerational issues within the organization, etc. (ii) Talent — the challenge is about how we attract good people and also creating opportunities to grow talent. (iii) Safety — creating a physically safe work environment. And (iv) social media — how do we increase our online presence and utilise the potential of social media to engage our customers?' says Martin.

Where does HR fit in this growth story? Martin was asked whether HR can be a change agent and play a leading role in solving challenges and sustaining businesses and, if so, how. He responds emphatically:

Yes, of course. HR can be a change agent. It's about earning a place at the table as a trusted advisor and business partner, and how we add value to the business bottom line and align ourselves with the business strategy. It is for this reason we recruit those who think 'retail first' and HR specialist second. As HR professionals we also have to identify and take care of people-related matters and HR risks such as legal compliance matters, bullying, social diversity and other safety, industrial relations and legal matters. The safety of our team members is our highest priority. We regularly monitor our safety performance and use measurements such as all injury and lost time injury frequency rates [AIFR and LTIFR; i.e., the occurrence of a medically treated injury or lost time injury per million hours worked] and take action on trends identified. We work closely with the business to establish safety systems that are aligned to our core values and risks and we train and educate all leaders and team members to equip them with the skills needed to work safely and to look out for each other. We not only ensure that our business is protected, but also that our team members remain safe.

Officeworks' 'Taking Care' strategy is essential for the company to become a sustainable business. The strategy clearly links the company's values about the environment, community, ethics and diversity and the way these values contribute to its financial success. Four important elements of the strategy are: (1) to produce environmentally friendly products and packaging; (2) to contribute towards children's education, health and well-being and local community groups as part of community initiatives; (3) to undertake business with integrity and treat both customers and suppliers with respect; (4) to offer a diverse and inclusive work environment where team members are given the support they need to learn and reach their potential. Over the years the company has taken a number of initiatives in this direction: for example, Officeworks partnered with the Australian Literacy and Numeracy Foundation to launch the inaugural 'Helping Kids Grow' campaign, which aims to help young, marginalised Australians realise their dreams and fulfil their potential (Questia, 2010); installation of the huge wind turbine dubbed the 'Green Power Tower' at Dandenong, Officeworks' largest store in Victoria, to generate energy to offset car park lighting costs; or teaming up with Fox FM to organise a series of outdoor events across the country as part of community initiatives (*Star News Group*, 2012). The company is well on track to becoming sustainable, is optimistic about its future and believes adaptability is the name of the game. It is embracing the challenges and 'taking care of big ideas at lowest prices'. In an interview given to the local media (*The Australian*, 2011), Officeworks Managing Director Mark Ward states:

. . . Retail's not dead. It's just changing a bit. There's a lot of doom and gloom about the future of stores and online taking over the world, but for me online is just another way to sell stuff, and retailers are adapting to that − some faster than others.

Case Study 4.5 Unilever Sri Lanka: 'Winning with People'

Incorporated in 1930, Unilever is a giant global fast-moving-and-consumer-goods (FMCG) company, with a social mission. Unilever's vision is to create a better future every day while helping people look good, feel good and get more out of life with brands and services that are good for them and good for others. The long history of the company is punctuated by many milestones: from launching one of the world's first packaged and branded grocery products, setting up advanced research and innovation centres, to unleashing the entrepreneurial spirit of rural women in many developing countries and thus changing lives. With more than 400 brands focussed on health and well-being and employing over 160,000 people in more than 180 countries, it touches the lives of over 2 billion people who use one of Unilever's products on any given day. In 2009 Unilever launched 'The Compass', its strategy for sustainable growth. The strategy has the following social mission:

> To work to create a better future every day, with brands and services that help people feel good, look good, and get more out of life; to lead for responsible growth, inspiring people to take small everyday actions that will add up to a big difference; developing new ways of doing business that will allow to double the size of the company, while reducing its environmental footprint and increasing positive social impact.
>
> (Unilever, 2013a and n.d.).

In 2013 this £50 billion company was ranked 39th in the World's Top-50 Most Admired Companies by *Fortune* (the global business magazine published by Time Inc.).

Unilever Sri Lanka (a subsidiary of Unilever Plc) was incorporated in 1938 and has had a great deal of influence on the social development of Sri Lanka. Unilever believes in 'doing well by doing good'. As one of the leading FMCG companies in Sri Lanka, the company has actively participated in many socioeconomic projects that include disaster relief assistance, facilitating economic independence among women in rural Sri Lanka by encouraging them to become micro-entrepreneurs, renovation of schools and Montessori[7] schools, drinking water and road development projects, renovation of community centres and construction of bridges (*DailyFT*, 2012). For instance, the company played a major role in post-2004 tsunami relief assistance and restructuring. Among the first few companies to respond spontaneously, Unilever Sri Lanka utilised its strong and deep island-wide distribution network to provide emergency relief operations, working alongside local agencies to distribute essential food and hygiene products to the affected. Initial relief work was followed by rehabilitation and reconstruction projects that included the rebuilding of 150 homes. The company also assisted the World Food Programme (WFP) in logistical support by chartering a train to deliver emergency food rations and medical supplies (Fernando, 2007).

Unilever Sri Lanka is presently home to 30 strong brands and over 200 products and provides employment to 1500 people directly and many thousands more indirectly through its dedicated suppliers, distributors and service providers (Unilever, 2013b). In his recent visit to Sri Lanka to inaugurate Unilever Sri Lanka's new manufacturing facility in Horana, Unilever Chief Executive Officer Paul Polman enthusiastically said:

> *I see a very different Sri Lanka today, compared to the one I saw last time, there is really nothing better than seeing peace and prosperity among people. I am also very happy to see the great strides Unilever Sri Lanka has made. I can see how far we have come over the last 75 years of our presence in Sri Lanka. However, this is only the beginning. I now want to see you compete with the best in the world, when it comes to efficiency, quality and overall excellence.*
>
> *(Unilever, 2012).*

In addition to the company's focus on growth and progress, what other business and HR challenges does the company face and how prepared is it to take on such challenges? Udayan Dutt, Director Human Resources and Corporate Relations, Unilever Sri Lanka says:

We are a huge global corporation. We are confronted with many business challenges like sustaining growth while getting into newer parts of the world, servicing markets well, bringing out newer products in line with the current context and changing consumer demand and ensuring growth by developing the market. On the people front, we have challenges to develop talent profile – to enable the right fit and designing the right organisational structure to drive growth and efficiency. As regards preparedness, it is an ongoing journey. We are a customer and consumer-centric company focussing on execution excellence. We are constantly looking into implementing better talent practices befitting changing consumer behaviour. We therefore bring in and develop talented individuals who are not only experts in their own domain but also understand the business and who can translate business requirements into a functional agenda and partner the business.

Unilever's business growth agenda is pretty straightforward in that it links performance with rewards, thereby enhancing productivity. The broad-based systematic approach to building a performance culture in the company called '3 + 1' is testimony to it. The '3 + 1' approach requires each employee to have 3 business goals and 1 development goal. Unilever has set a goal of turbocharging a performance culture in the company. This is about setting out a clear direction on key priorities and identifying KPIs. The outcomes of employees' actions are assessed against results, with performance measured on a yearly basis and rated on a 1 to 5 scale. Performance ratings and potential are linked to the achievement of targets demonstrating competencies and values and employees are rewarded based on their own performance and that of the business. Linkages between performance and reward are communicated to the employees on a regular basis through performance scorecards, quality checks, performance rating and talent potential awareness (Dutt, 2013). As Udayan notes:

> Our reward strategy is aligned to our business objectives. We believe that rewards can be used to drive the objectives of the organisation. Our reward strategy focuses on four key areas: (a) pay for performance − rewarding employees based on their performance; (b) strategically aligned total rewards − to see if our business and operative objectives are attained; (c) market competition − by focusing on reward opportunities, peer groups and position of fixed elements [nondiscretionary compensation that does not vary according to performance or results achieved. It usually is determined by the organization's pay philosophy and structure.] and (d) ease of understanding and delivery − understanding the reward mechanism and its contribution to the organisation's success.

Having put the performance goals in place, the company sets about supporting its employees by working out multiple training programmes that help employees achieve their goals. For instance, in an effort to improve workforce performance, Unilever Sri Lanka in association with the Sri Lanka Institute of Marketing (SLIM) launched a 9-month Professional Selling diploma course for sales representatives/ frontline staff employed by the company's distribution business partners and service providers, who operate in all areas of the country (*Business Times*, 2013).

Unilever believes that it has to have a diverse and inclusive workforce for its business growth agenda to be effective (Unilever Careers, 2012). For instance:

> 'When I think of diversity, I think of an organisation that has the best talent and taps into all the possible sources we have, be it gender, race, qualifications, etc. and employs the best, the most appropriate talent that is required for Unilever to succeed. One of the biggest challenges in building a diverse organisation comes when you have a non-diverse talent mix to begin with, where, if left unchecked, the tendency to recruit and develop those who are similar becomes popular. Breaking this mindset and bringing in the enabling processes that encourage diversity become the most important challenges for any organisation dedicated to creating an inclusive workplace. A few enabling actions in that direction include recruiting and developing women managers, creating a more flexible and agile working culture for a better work−life balance, allowing working from home as an option for our employees and helping build the future women leaders in business by putting in place strong mentoring programmes for students. There is still a long way for us to go, but we have already started the journey and should be getting there soon!' says Udayan.

With top leadership from 21 nations and more than 30 per cent of managers worldwide being women (Unilever, 2008), Unilever is one of the world's most culturally diverse companies. A diverse and inclusive workforce creates a more positive work environment, which increases productivity and contributes to sustainable, profitable growth.

Building on Unilever's heritage of combining its social mission with commercial success, the company set itself the global objective of doubling its size and reducing its environmental footprint at the same time. In 2010 Unilever put in place the 'Unilever Sustainable Living Plan' (USLP), which committed the company to a 10-year journey towards sustainable growth. The USLP only sanctions company growth if there is no environmental impact and, in this way, enhances its social impact at the same time. It has set itself three major goals to achieve by 2020: (1) to improve the health and well-being of Sri Lankans; (2) to reduce the environmental impact of the company; (3) to source 100 per cent of agricultural raw materials sustainably and enhance the livelihoods of people across the value chain (Unilever, 2013a). As part of the USLP, the company has partnered with the Sri Lankan Ministry of Health to improve hygiene practices and help the ministry conduct a hygiene awareness campaign among pregnant women on the importance of proper hand washing (The Island, 2012).

When asked what roles HR can play and is playing in achieving the objectives of the USLP, Udayan emphasises:

HR has to stay two steps ahead by proactively engaging itself at the early stages of formulation of business strategies and plans, make sense of it, interpret it in people terms, equip line managers with necessary tools and support in the execution of business goals.

With eyes firmly set on goals, processes intact and enthusiasm charged, it is timely that Unilever Sri Lanka is now receiving awards and rewards. Unilever Sri Lanka won four awards at the Effies 2012 for marketing effectiveness and great execution. The Effie Awards were established by the American Marketing Association and introduced in Sri Lanka through the SLIM (the national body of marketers). In 2012 Unilever Sri Lanka was ranked Most Preferred Employer amongst undergraduates in a survey conducted by Taylor Nelson Sofres (TNS). It was also ranked No. 1 FMCG company and Most Respected Multinational Company in Sri Lanka by LMD (the Sri Lanka business magazine). For its commitment and contribution towards creating a better future for all in Sri Lanka, Unilever was selected by the Ceylon Chamber of Commerce as one of the Ten Best Corporate Citizens in the nation for 2012 (Unilever, 2013a, p. 1). Unilever Sri Lanka won Gold at the HRM Awards 2012 organized by the Association of Human Resource Professionals, in collaboration with Aon Hewitt. Unilever also received the Category Award for Best Practices in the Reward and Recognition category. Udayan (*Daily Mirror*, 2012) states:

We are delighted to be recognized by the Association of HR Professionals as one of the best employers in Sri Lanka with world-class HR practices. Unilever has long since known that having people with the right talent, skills and creativity is crucial for the sustained growth of the company. With a wealth of global knowledge on employee relations, training and development, Unilever is proud to be a pioneer in the market in terms of people management and administration processes.

With strong local roots and access to global expertise, Unilever Sri Lanka is right on track for 'Winning with People'.

Case Study 4.6 Nokia India: 'Connecting People through Innovation and Adapting to Change'

Founded in 1865, Nokia is a multinational communications and information technology corporation that evolved from being a riverside paper mill in southwest Finland to a global telecommunications leader connecting over 1.3 billion people through its innovative products (Nokia, 2012a, p. 7). With a total global workforce of over 97,000 spread across 120 countries, sales in over 150 countries, annual revenues of around €30 billion (US$39 billion approximately), its global market share is 22.5 per cent (Nokia, 2013, p. 39; BBC, 2012). The company has put in place a three-pronged strategy to enable it to adapt to the changing business environment and grow sustainably: (1) to deliver industry-leading smartphones (by partnering with Microsoft to use the Windows Phone operating system); (2) to bring the full benefits of mobile communications to consumers with limited economic means and increase its global consumer base from 1.3 billion to 2 billion; (3) to focus on future disruptions in technology [An innovation that creates a new market by applying a different set of values, which ultimately (and unexpectedly) overtakes an existing market Christensen (1997).], business and process areas that have been identified as having a profound influence on the telecommunications industry (Nokia, 2012a, p. 5).

Retail for Nokia is still at an early stage in India. Nokia started its operations in India in 1995 and entered three broad business sectors: mobile phones, multimedia and enterprise. Initially employing 450 people, the number has now grown to around 6000 (BusinessMapsofIndia.com, n.d.). Nokia's innovative and price-sensitive products have made it a household name and the company has emerged as the most trusted brand in India (Ladage, 2013).

Sustainability is an important part of Nokia's business strategy. The company systematically and regularly analyses ways to engage stakeholders and has found that harnessing sustainability-related opportunities is one means of doing this. For instance, in 2011 Nokia decided to create an organisational atmosphere in which health and safety were considered top priorities at its factory in Chennai (India). Comprehensive plant safety audits and machinery risk assessments were conducted and factory-level targets were defined and embedded within the performance management system to ensure accountability (Nokia, 2013, p. 33).

Nokia does much more than connect and engage with people, it also cares for them by looking after their health and well-being as well as improving the quality of education they receive. For instance, it partnered with Arogya World (a US-based non-profit organization set up to eliminate chronic disease in India one community at a time) and other partners to inform one million Indians about diabetes prevention (Nokia, 2012b, p. 25; Arogya World, 2013). On the education front, the company has developed Nokia Education Delivery, freely download-able open-source software, which works on Nokia devices with Windows, Symbian and S40 operating systems carrying high-quality educational material to mobile phones via mobile networks. Owing to its success in providing access to high-quality educational material for all and sundry at any time, Nokia Education Delivery was awarded the Best Education Service by the UK *Computer Active* magazine at the Mobile World Congress in Barcelona 2012 (Nokia, 2012b, p. 1).

As part of its responsibility towards the environment, the company has under-taken a number of green initiatives, such as: (1) supporting the conservation project of the International Union for Conservation of Nature (IUCN) in the Indian Himalayas; (2) helping communities in the region learn how water management can be used to build climate resilience and (3) partnering with NGOs, schools, colleges, government bodies and corporations to highlight the importance of recycling phones and accessories as well as providing incentives for the same (Nokia, 2012b, p. 56). During 2011, some 1.2 million phones and accessories (weighing over 60 tonnes) were collected for responsible recycling. In addition, Nokia India planted approximately 36,000 trees during 2011 in cooperation with Humana People to People India (HPPI), World Alliance for Youth Empowerment, Rotary Midtown Bangalore and GrowTrees.com.

Nokia has its own unique ways not only of engaging with consumers and stake-holders but also keeping them interested in the progress of the company. For instance, it recently teamed up with New India Assurance (the Indian government-owned insurance company) to offer customers insurance cover against any loss of or damage to their handsets. Nokia's insurance plan provides cover against burglary, theft and accidental damage, such as when the handset is accidentally immersed in water (CyberMedia, 2013; BBC, 2012).

Healthcare industry

Healthcare is one of the world's largest and fastest growing industries. The health and well-being of a nation's workforce has major significance for that nation's economy. Our case study of GlaxoSmithKline (GSK) China indicates this signifi-cance, takes a look at the challenges the industry is facing and points out a number of ways to sustain growth.

Case Study 4.7 GSK China: 'Helping People to Do More, Feel Better and Live Longer'

Global healthcare company GSK's three primary areas of business are pharmaceuticals, vaccines and consumer healthcare. It employs more than 99,000 people world-wide (GSK, 2013a). Despite the company starting operations on 1 January 2001 following the merger of GlaxoWellcome plc and SmithKline Beecham plc, its history can be traced back to the 1700s. GSK invests heavily in research to develop new medicines, vaccines and innovative consumer products. It is one of the few healthcare companies entrusted by the World Health Organisation (WHO) to research and develop medicines and vaccines for HIV/AIDS, tuberculosis and malaria, the WHO's three priority diseases. Headquartered in London, the company has a turnover of £26.4 billion. It has a presence in more than 115 countries and major research centres in the UK, US, Spain, Belgium and China (GSK, 2013a,b).

GSK entered the Chinese market in 2001, though its parent companies had been operating there since 1908. As the largest multinational pharmaceutical enterprise in China, GSK has a total investment of over US$500 million; six operating companies comprising American Tianjin Smith Kline Pharmaceutical (joint venture), GlaxoSmithKline (Tianjin) (joint venture), GlaxoSmithKline Pharmaceuticals (Suzhou), Shanghai GlaxoSmithKline Biologicals, GlaxoSmithKline Biologicals (Shenzhen) and Nanjing Pharmaceutical Camry; more than 5000 employees and a state-of-the-art global R&D centre that focusses on neurosciences (GSK-China, 2013). GSK opened a new research unit in 2012 to look at traditional Chinese medicine (TCM). The unit has been working with TCM experts to develop new, innovative and differentiated products that incorporate the best of traditional and modern medicines (Wang, 2012). The potential in this area is huge, but resources need to be invested and the business risks and challenges addressed. The potential benefits for healthcare are immense.

To achieve the strategic business objectives of 'helping people to do more, feel better and live longer', GSK's focus has been on creating an inclusive, engaging environment that empowers employees by keeping them healthy so that their contribution to the organisation is uninterrupted by periods of ill health. For instance, in 2012 the company piloted the Preventative Health Programme, designed to improve the quality of life of GSK's employees and their families. The programme, planned to be rolled out globally, helped reduce the employee injury and illness rate by 10 per cent. With the aim of 'zero harm to our people', GSK continues to develop risk reduction programmes like upgrades to guard equipment on machinery and dust reduction activities in manufacturing sites (GSK, 2012).

GSK recognises HR as a core asset. The company's business model is based on the use of knowledge and the development of intellectual property, which are largely people driven. Key to the sustainability of their businesses is the ability of the workforce to come up with newer innovative products (GSK, 2012). The three strategic priorities of GSK are improving growth, reducing risk and improving long-term financial performance. The company's Corporate Responsibility Committee is tasked with safeguarding and enhancing long-term shareholder value and providing a robust platform to realise the group's strategy. In 2013 the Corporate Responsibility Committee's focus was on four core themes which the committee believed reflects the most important issues for responsible and sustainable business growth:

i. *Health for all*: innovating newer products to address currently unmet health needs; improving access to their products, irrespective of where people live or their ability to pay; and controlling or eliminating diseases affecting the world's most vulnerable people.

ii. *Behaviour*: putting the interests of patients and consumers first; making sure that everything they do is driven by such values as respect for others, putting the patient at the centre and treating the patient in an open, transparent, decent and honest way; and backing everything up by robust policies and strong compliance processes.

iii. *People*: enabling people to thrive and develop as individuals and in so doing deliver their mission.

iv. *Planet*: growing their business while reducing the environmental impact across the value chain. Environmental sustainability is a priority for GSK. The company has set ambitious targets to reduce carbon, water and waste by changing the way raw materials are used and advising consumers on the use and disposal of company products (GSK, 2012, p. 108).

Despite the recent GSK China debacle in which the UK drug maker was convicted of having bribed doctors and hospitals to promote its own products and got itself fined US$490 million in the process, it is actively engaged in a number of initiatives focussed on responsible and sustainable business growth in areas like health education, public health, medical education, donations to schools, disaster assistance, investment funds, medicines and equipment. These initiatives are worth in excess of RMB250 million (GSK-China, 2013).

Andrew Witty, Chief Executive GSK, best sums up the group's thought processes and future priorities (Langreth, 2011; GSK, 2012; *The Telegraph*, 2013):

> *This industry is under huge pressure. There is no point in dreaming about being in a different world. We have to change. We have diversified our sources of growth, our R&D productivity has significantly improved and our processes are simpler and more efficient. We are confident that our strategy is delivering. But as with any organisation there is inevitably a vulnerability to people working outside systems. If that is the case [in China] that clearly is going to raise questions over how you can control for that. My unrelenting focus is on getting controls right and building a culture and values that protect us from corruption. But I am absolutely sure a massive 99.9 per cent of people in GSK understands the rules and values of the organisation.*

Education

According to a recent report published by UNESCO, 84 per cent of the world's adult (15 years and older) population is literate, but 774 million are illiterate. The significance of the education sector is well articulated in this quote by the Secretary General of the Organisation for Economic Co-operation and Development (OECD) Angel Gurría, when she says:

> *Knowledge and skills are the most valuable assets to present and future generations, as governments seek to maintain global competitiveness, increase the flexibility and responsiveness of labour markets and deal with issues of population ageing.*

During the course of our research, we interviewed Rajeev Kumar, Vice Chair of the International Association of Business Communicators (IABC) Global Communication Certification Council and Regional Manager of Media at Tata Group Corporate Affairs and Media. Previously actively involved with a number of academic institutions, he says:

There is a need for faculty with greater commitment to the [education] profession. Let me comment on India-specific challenges. Getting top-quality faculty is a major challenge and retaining them is another. While the number of institutions offering education has multiplied, regular full-time faculty of quality is confined to a few accredited institutions. This is also because pay scales of faculty are relatively much less than what corporate scales pay. Many prefer to be adjunct or visiting faculty as it gives them freedom to work in more than one place. So, one good reason is the economic reason. Quality is also impacted by the low-quality PhD degrees awarded by some institutions. It may also be that while some PhD degree holders are well grounded in research, they lack instructional abilities and hence their performance in the classroom is found wanting. Faculty management is a challenge. There is a need for more investment in faculty. By this I mean not only competitive remuneration but also an investment in their development. There is also a need for mentoring new faculty as well as a need for reverse mentoring of old faculty by the new. Faculty integration poses a challenge as the generation gap is experienced in this domain also. Where ego is given more value, cooperation amongst faculty suffers. In some academic/training institutions, the performance-related variable in compensation is put in place. This indirectly introduces rivalry amongst faculty members and affects overall efficiency of the institution. Overall, I believe in the education sector. Attrition is a risk. Retention is the challenge. Engagement is the solution.

He goes on to say:

There is a need to design curricula for industry-specific needs so that once a student finishes an academic course he or she is ready for the specific industry. Though industry-specific courses are emerging – the curriculum of which is designed in consultation with a specific industry, there is still far greater scope for industry–academia interaction. An institution must have a guiding philosophy of education to which all faculty members are committed. At the Goa Institute of Management, we adopted an education philosophy keeping in view its long-term vision and benchmarking practices against the world's best management institutions. This philosophy was drafted by me and we went through a process of co-creation of the philosophy through constant discussion and debate between faculty members and the board that governed the institution. The final document that was adopted by the board was then owned by all faculty members and became the guiding document for growth of the institution and the practices that it would follow in the coming decades. Executive education is also a challenge. The quality of executive education suffers when content is not a good mix of theory and practice. There is a need for faculty to be exposed to both academics and industry so that they offer pragmatic education to executives. It is also observed that while the corporate sector invests in learning and development activities, the quality of executive education is not monitored and very little of what is learnt in short workshops gets carried forward to the workplace. Executive education is big business especially for independent consultants and trainers who try and develop long-term personal relations with top organisational staff of corporate organisations and continue to offer substandard programs and care little for feedback from trainees.

The challenges facing the education sector are intriguing and it will take time for them to be properly addressed. Case Study 4.8, which deals with Tata Group, shows how heritage and innovation can go hand in hand and be of benefit for the education sector.

Case study 4.8 Tata Group: 'Bridging Heritage and Innovation in the Education Sector'

Tata Group was founded in 1868 by Jamsetji Nusserwanji Tata. The highly successful Indian conglomerate has over 100 operating companies, 32 publicly listed enterprises, a shareholder base of 3.8 million, an overall employee base of over 450,000 and a huge global presence (85 countries around the world). The group operates in seven diverse business sectors: information technology and communications, engineering products and services, materials, services, energy, consumer products and chemicals (Tata Sons, 2013a). Tata Group is unique in the way it is controlled by Tata philanthropic trusts through their 66 per cent majority stake in Tata Sons, which in turn is the biggest shareholder in each of the Tata companies. The trusts are a conglomeration of two big and many smaller units, the first of which was set up in 1919 and named after Ratan Tata, the younger son of the group's founder. Before he died in 1918, he bequeathed all his personal wealth to philanthropy. Since then, the family has donated its wealth in the company to the trusts (Mukherjee Saha & Rowley, 2013, p. 37). The family-owned conglomerate, which turns over US$100 billion, is widely known for its value system, ethics and commitment to the community. Tata companies and Tata trusts are long-term supporters of social causes, community projects and academic institutions. They believe in giving back to society what came from society and work in the areas of health, education, women and child development, training of young adults and building sustainable livelihoods and environmental conservation (Tata Sons, 2013b). The group has been seamlessly carrying out its more than century-old heritage of leadership based on trust and integrity. Today, Tata Group is among the world's top-40 most valuable brands with a brand valuation of US$18.16 billion (Brand Finance, 2013).

The Tata Group keeps a constant focus on innovation, which helps it deliver breakthrough products/services and propel it through the changing dynamism of global business. In June 2007 the Tata Group Innovation Forum (TGIF) was formed with the express purpose of stimulating innovative thinking, encouraging innovation and creating an innovative environment and culture in Tata companies. Tata InnoVerse is one of TGIF's noteworthy initiatives in which the essence of karma is promoted. InnoVerse is a web-based open innovation platform through which every employee in Tata's companies spread around the world gets karma points as a result of posting an idea, commenting on it right through to implementing it (TQMS, 2010). This system promotes the culture of innovation and provides opportunities for the cross-pollination of ideas across the group's companies. The karma of employees is rewarded not only financially but they get a chance to partner in the legacy the group leaves behind as well. Tata Swach, a low-cost water purifier, is just one of many examples of such karma-focussed collaborative innovation where companies in Tata Group came together to put ideas into action. The Tata Swach water purifier uses advanced nanotechnology and has received more awards than any other water purifier in the world (Mukherjee Saha & Rowley, 2013, p. 37; Tata Chemicals, 2012).

When Ratan Tata retired as head of Tata Group in 2012, he handed over responsibility of steering the group to the incoming Chairman of Tata Group Cyrus Mistry and in so doing brought about change at the highest level in the group. While Ratan Tata's successful era of leadership could be attributed to such sectors as IT and communications, engineering, automobiles and materials, the era of Cyrus Mistry may well be driven by success in the education sector. Tata Group has identified the education sector as a thrust area driving its future growth over the next decade (Manghat, 2011).

In an article published in the *Tata Review*, the education sector was identified as the next big opportunity:

> The education life cycle consists of five segments: pre-school, kindergarten to Class XII (K12), higher education (graduation and post-graduation), vocational/ career training and corporate training. There are various types of education providers with different objectives. Each of these segments is expected to undergo significant structural changes, throwing up new opportunities for the private sector
> *(Raman & Ganguli, 2010).*

Tata Review is a quarterly magazine that, in its own words, 'seeks to establish the Tata Group's thought leadership by featuring the views of the top management on issues of contemporary significance and articulating the group's vision of the future.'

The Tata Management Training Centre (TMTC) was set up by the legendary J. R. D. Tata in 1966. TMTC is the world's second oldest corporate university and was tasked with being an educational institution that would assist, foster, cultivate and contribute to the development of professional management for the economic development of the country (Smedley, 2013). TMTC's vision, as the learning arm of Tata Group, is to help develop leaders, rejuvenate the group's leadership pipeline, and nurture the Tata talent pool. Each year, the campus plays host to some 10,000 senior Tata executives (Rao, 2013). TMTC provides unique learning solutions at the intersection between academia and practice.

Historically, Tata Group has always emphasised the significance of education for society and contributed in many ways to this sector. Founder of Tata Group Jamsetji N. Tata said:

> ... what advances a nation or the community is not so much to prop up its weakest and most helpless members, but to lift up the best and the most gifted, so as to make them of the greatest service to the country. I prefer this constructive philanthropy which seeks to educate and develop the faculties of the best of our young men.

From establishing the J. N. Tata Endowment Scholarship in 1892 and providing loans for talented Indian youngsters to pursue an education abroad (Tata Sons, 2013b, p. 1), to donating US$50 million to the Harvard Business School (the largest donation received from an international donor in its history) in support of the school's educational mission to mould the next generation of global business leaders (HBS, 2010), the group has always acted according to the founder's philosophy.

The group has taken many initiatives over the years to improve the quality of education in India. It set up iconic institutions like the Indian Institute of Science (IISc), the Tata Institute of Social Sciences (TISS) and Tata Institute of Fundamental Research (TIFR), in addition to establishing many scholarship funds. For instance, in 2003 Tata Steel set up the Tata Steel Education Excellence Programme (TEEP) to promote excellence in education at schools in areas where the company has operations. Based on the Baldrige Education Excellence Model (BEEM), the objective of this initiative was to improve the quality of education, create a culture of excellence and nurture the citizens of tomorrow. Teachers and principals undergo training to become assessors who look at schools participating in the programme once a year (Wadia, 2011). To make education a fun and interesting experience, Tata Interactive, a subsidiary of Tata Group, launched ClassEdge, a cloud-based, multimedia, collaborative education solution for Indian schools. The solution, which includes a state-of-the-art projection system and an MPLS (multiprotocol label switching) connection, is hosted on Tata's servers and made available to schools on a subscription basis. Such an education model is expected to help children with learning disabilities as well (Shreshtha, 2011).

Tata Group has undertaken many initiatives for skill-based education and training to be made accessible to youngsters in India, especially the underprivileged. Taj Hotels Resorts and Palaces, a subsidiary of Tata Group, has tied up with several government Industrial Training Institutes (ITIs) in rural India to offer skill-based training to local youngsters. The group helps the institutes update their curricula and make them relevant to the job market, facilitates the infrastructure required for the training programmes and helps students find internship opportunities. The group is also a key member of the national advisory team of the MoT's *Hunar-Se-Rozgar Tak* project, which has the objective of training and facilitating the creation of employable skills amongst youngsters from economically weaker strata of society (Menon, 2011). TISS is the first school teaching social science in India. It has recently signed an agreement with the All India Council for Technical

Education (AICTE) to set up a national vocational school. This collaboration between TISS and the AICTE is expected to create a climate in which sustainable sources of income are available to marginalized youngsters and industry can grow as a result of being provided skilled HR (TISS, 2013).

Tata Group's aspiration is to become a truly global entity while adhering to the group's belief in long-term stakeholder value creation, as made clear by Chairman Emeritus Ratan Tata:

> One hundred years from now, I expect Tata Group to be much bigger, of course, than it is now. More importantly, I hope the group comes to be regarded as being the best in India — best in the manner in which we operate, best in the products we deliver and best in our value system and ethics.

Such an aspiration rests on having skilled human resources that are fully attuned to a continually changing global dynamism. The group's involvement in the education and training sector is key to achieving the next level of growth.

Energy

Economic activity quite simply depends on the energy industry. The significance of the energy industry has already been discussed (see Chapters 1–3). In this section two case studies are presented as examples of how energy companies are dealing with human resources and at the same time energising both their own organisations and the industry in which they operate.

Case Study 4.9 AMR India: 'Growing with Confidence'

AMR Group is a public, limited, fast-growing business conglomerate with businesses in core sectors such as mining, construction, infrastructure and energy. Incorporated in 1992 as a partnership, the group has come a long way towards its vision 'to be the most admired global infrastructure and mining company for its performance'. The construction division of the company is engaged in building factories, house building, roads, site grading[8] and related infrastructure work. It has successfully carried out a number of civil work projects in India and Nepal. As a result of its expertise in mining techniques, equipment, flexibility in operations and systems, AMR holds a leading position in the Indian mining industry. Its annual mining capacity is in excess of 65 million tonnes. Operating in the mineral-rich belt of India, it is engaged in extracting minerals such as limestone, coal and lignite. AMR's infrastructure division is engaged in areas like survey, investigation and design; excavation and embankment (construction of the structures involved and the spraying of concrete linings); earthen dams; and barrages. The energy division concentrates on providing services in the transmission and distribution of energy to rural sectors, while looking to expand in renewable energy.

An employee base in excess of 1500, a yearly turnover of Rs 1200 crore (approximately US$19,657,189), reaching the standard required for ISO 9001:2000 certification and receiving the International Excellence Award for Construction Quality and Design in 2008 are testimony to AMR Group's success. The group has grown rapidly and scaled new heights. Its venture into warehousing in semi-urban and rural markets has been far reaching. The group is known for its strong financial discipline and modern management practices, which have made it one of the most admired companies in its field (AMR, 2013).

What are the business and people challenges facing such a high-growth company when it ventures into competitive markets?

> 'We need to think long term and not just worry about short-term benefits. We need to ensure that the business process owners incorporate long-term issues into the financial model while bidding for projects. We are in a tough job, mostly in remote locations. So another challenge is availability of right skills matching our business models, compensation and job profile,' explains Manoj Kumar Sharma, group Senior Vice President HR.

How prepared are they to handle such challenges?

> 'We are gearing up by putting the right business processes in place, using our past industry-specific experiences and taking calculated risks. AMR has carved out a niche in the mining business and formed A&M Resources Private Limited – a JV with Assent Trade and Investment Private Limited [ATIP], Mauritius in May 2011. A&M is relatively young company and have just begun our journey, we are taking the buy-in from client organisations (that include government, quasi-government and reputed Indian companies and corporations) at each stage and making them equally realise the pain points. We constantly communicate with our stakeholders on all critical issues and try to resolve matters mutually,' notes Manoj.

When asked what role HR can play in dealing with industry-specific business dynamisms, Manoj confidently says:

> Even when the three Ms [money (finance), materials (resources) and machines (technology)] fail, we keep ticking. HR has always been a front-runner – of course, we work together with the business head and CEO. HR has a key role to play – be it providing solutions to the functional heads in good or bad times and work together protecting the business's bottom line, revising key result areas (KRAs), communicating fact-based/data-backed business reality, handling situations of rightsizing or optimising overstaffing that may have occurred as a result of some negligence in the process or compulsion, strategies for retaining high poten-tials to sustain business operations, charting cost-effective compensation strategies, protecting the interest of the stakeholders, managing HR risks like arresting rumours among employees and other stakeholders and more.

Despite AMR Group concentrating on growing its business, social responsibility is not only high on its agenda but the group further believes it to be a continuous process. To serve society and the broader community, the group has recently established the AMR Foundation. The foundation extends financial support to needy students to help them pursue their studies and provides medical expenses to poor and needy patients. It has also recently organised a charity event to promote and support hockey (the oft-ignored but de facto national sport of India) (Hamara Photos, 2010).

> 'We are also environmentally conscious. We abide by the Mines Rules and Regulations under the regulatory authority of DGMS, India. As a law-abiding organisation, it is our obligation to comply with the norms of all the statutory authorities regulating the businesses. My previous organisation has put up a 40 MW solar power plant in Gujarat and also earned carbon credits for our coal-based supercritical technology power plant (STPP). In fact, the mining and energy industry in India is progressing and taking many green initiatives for the greater good. In one of my previous organisations, I had an additional portfolio of handling the function of environment. I was management representative (MR) for ISO 14000 and handled statutory compliances of state government on environment. I remember receiving complaints from society alleging wilful emissions of either polluted water or gases from our chimneys. I had taken the challenge on both fronts: (a) bringing awareness in society that such emissions are not harming and much below the limits set by the government and (b) making our employees aware of their responsibilities towards society and country at large. I invited the local municipal body members and other government officials to our plant, took them around the cold-rolling steel plant, showing them the technological and systems initiatives taken by the organisation. I personally used to visit the company-made ponds, where our plant water was discharged to see to my satisfaction that fishes and other creatures live like in fresh water. It was the testimony of our obligation as a citizen of our country. I strongly feel that HR has a role in safekeeping the environment through education − bringing awareness among employees, society, investors and government officials for informing them about the new initiatives being taken in this direction and encouraging them to be part of it, ensuring the good environmental practices like conserving water, energy, recycling, etc. are recognised and rewarded,' concludes Manoj.

Case Study 4.10 JK Organisation: cementing its century-old 'Caring for People' tradition

JK Organisation (FZ) is one of India's largest business houses, founded more than 125 years ago and run by the Singhania family. The company is an industrial conglomerate that employs more than 30,000 and has an annual turnover exceeding US$4 billion. It is involved in many areas such as automotive tyres and tubes (JK Tyre); paper and pulp (JK Paper); cement (JK Lakshmi Cement); aerospace, defence and security (ADS) (Global Strategic Technologies); power transmission systems (Fenner); hybrid seeds (JK Agri Genetics); sugar (JK Sugar); food and dairy products (Umang Dairies); and clinical research (ClinRX). It has a strong global presence with manufacturing operations and outsourcing arrangements in different parts of the world and exports to more than 60 countries in 6 continents (JKO, 2012).

JK Organisation (EZ) is known for its employee-friendly work environment. Caring for people, integrity (including intellectual honesty, openness, fairness and trust) and commitment to excellence are the core values cementing its century-old people-friendly tradition. When asked whether he thinks HR could be a game changer, Dilep Misra, President and Head Corporate Human Resources at JK Organisation states:

> *The highly diversified JK Group has a unique and power forum of central HRD [human resource development] committee which is headed by the group chairman and attended by all directors, business heads, corporate HR and business HR heads and senior executives. The committee has four calendarised full-day meetings during the year, one each quarter, with a predetermined and focussed HR agenda. The committee debates and approves all major corporate HR initiatives. So, HR at JK has been playing a game-changing role by being a business partner and a strategic player. Corporate HR is involved in all business-planning exercises while assisting to improve productivity and meet business bottom lines.*

The organisation has won a number of awards on the back of its good HR practices. Two that the company is particularly proud of are the Great Place to Work Award and the Confederation of Indian Industry's (CII) Strong Commitment to HR Excellence 2011 Award.

Ever since 2003, JKO (EZ) has implemented a competency-based, integrated HR system that has a strong focus on talent management and leadership development. It is one of the very few organisations in India to include *learnability* as a critical competency for the future:

> '*In our organisation, we help employees develop through mentoring and coaching. We have always believed in the role of developing leaders to create a high-performance organisation. One of our notable practices being our Krishna–Arjuna program,' explains Dilep.*

The Krishna–Arjuna concept of mentoring at JK Group is driven by the belief that when Krishna (the Supreme Personality of Godhead and the mentor of Arjuna) and Arjuna (finest archer, unrivalled warrior and high performer), the heroes of the Hindu epic *Mahabharata* instrumental in winning the great mythological battle of *Kurukshetra*, come together, then victory is certain.

Organisation-wide sustainable change is brought about by assessing Arjunas (identified high performers) and by developing individual development plans (IDPs), put together by external experts and internal HR leaders, for Arjunas to use in consultation with their Krishnas (mentors). In an effort to improve leadership competencies, the Krishnas give Arjunas challenging developmental assignments for them to complete on the job so that identified leadership competencies like analysis, decision making, learnability, communication and business perspective can be developed. The Arjunas share their experiences of the learning journey with their Krishnas. The corporate HRD team reviews the progress of the Arjunas each month and the best Krishna−Arjuna teams are congratulated periodically. Based on 360-degree and competency assessment feedback, the behaviour of senior leaders is identified for coaching (Bhide, 2011). Experienced external coaches are engaged to look at such behaviour and help develop an individual's leadership skills. Dilep has been instrumental in setting up an initiative to develop a coaching culture in the group. This has involved putting together a team of internal master coaches.

Innovation and passion to perform have always been the driving forces at JK and the group fosters intrapreneurs at all levels. In a recent media interview, Dilep elaborates:

We believe that all employees need varied skills, resources and competencies to help flourish their ideas. Thus, the company, at the recruitment level, begins identifying these personnel against the 12 leadership competencies based on 3 core concepts of business, self and people management. They are then identified as emerging leaders, business leaders or top leaders and encouraged to pursue innovative ideas. Under the policy Udaan, *the organisation identifies cross-functional teams that work on business ideas and their implementation. The winning team has the opportunity to implement their idea across varied business functions. Through this, we look to foster innovation in times of uncertainty.*

Nevertheless, Dilep emphasises much remains to be done because of the looming challenges of talent acquisition and retention:

In India, there is now a scarcity of talent. The industry is growing very fast but many talents have migrated out of the country. There is a gap between supply and demand of talent at market place. Also, with the growth of the IT industry and perceived lucrative jobs in the IT industry, youths are more attracted towards IT than other relatively traditional industries. Also, with employees' growing focus on monetary benefits, talent retention is, at times, a challenge.

Fully aware of the importance of grooming the right talent and the possibility of backward integration of talent, the company has set up a number of educational institutions at all levels: from the primary to post-graduate and doctorate level. The JK Lakshmipat University, a private university in Rajasthan, is a prime example. In addition, financial assistance is provided to various bodies engaged in delivering quality education and training. The organisation has taken adult literacy and women education initiatives in rural areas to equip people with basic education. Known as 'the Classroom with a Difference', the adult literacy programme through its 149 centres across the country reaches out to many people. This initiative is at the heart of the group's endeavour to help the deprived and less fortunate become literate, self-employed and self-reliant. The story of a tribal woman, proudly narrated by the JK team who took part in the initiative, demonstrates the impact of the programme:

> The tribal woman went to the bank to withdraw money from her account. She signed the slip but the teller did not hand over the money as her thumb impression did not match her signature. She completely refused to give her thumb impression now that she was literate. Instead, she walked back to her village, 14 kilometres away, brought the certificate that JK had given her and her Election Commission Identity Card. Her new ID was created. She put in so much effort simply to prove that she was literate. She is now a confident and self-reliant person.

The organisation is genuine in its efforts to give back to society by means of structured corporate social responsibility initiatives, not only in the field of education and adult literacy but also in health, the environment, social infrastructure and sport. For instance, in Rayagada (Orissa), JK Paper Mills has embarked on an innovative pilot project to respond to climate change and sustainable development. In an area with a predominately tribal population, low literacy and high unemployment, the mill distributes saplings to locals at subsidised rates, trains and encourages them to grow and maintain the trees, thereby generating an income stream for locals while conserving nature. In the last five years, over 100,000 saplings have been planted (Worldwatch Institute, 2013). Dilep notes:

> We give a lot of emphasis on energy efficiency and green practices. We envisage making the organisation paperless and integrating such factors with our performance management system.

JK Organisation has won several awards and most of the group's plants have ISO 9001 certification and some have also earned QS 9000 and ISO 14001 certifications, which deal with environmental concerns. The JK Tyre plant at Kankroli was the first tyre company in Asia and the second in the world to receive the ISO 50001:2011 energy management system certification awarded by the British Standards Institution.

The organisation is led by Hari Shankar Singhania, its president. A visionary and one of the most respected business leaders in India, he received the prestigious Padma Bhushan Award (the third highest civilian award in India) in 2003 for his contributions to Indian national and international business (*Hindustan Times*, 2012).

In 2005 he received the Royal Order of the Polar Star, one of Sweden's highest honours, from the King of Sweden, for his contribution to the development of Indo-Swedish business relations. He articulates the group's philosophy in the following way:

> *Excellence comes not from mere words or procedures. It comes from an urge to strive and deliver the best. A mindset that says, when it is good enough, improve it. It is a way of thinking that comes only from a power within.*

Conclusion

This chapter presents ten case studies of organisations (Table 4.1) in specific industries in the region. It examines how they have dealt with challenges facing not only their respective businesses but their HR as well. Interviews with experts from our focus industries are also given. This provides substantial evidence on what (and the extent to which) HR should be focussing on to help sustain the growth of industries across the GAPAC region (the subject matter of Chapter 5).

Notes

1. ASEAN stands for the Association of Southeast Asian Nations.
2. Physical invigoration is the activity of improving one's vitality and vigour.
3. Mental rejuvenation is activity that renews one's health and spirits by enjoyment and relaxation.
4. A tourist circuit is a route on which at least three major tourist destinations are located such that none is in the same town, village or city.
5. A tourist facilitator is someone conducting business for providing services for planning and arranging all-inclusive tour packages for tourists, either fixed tour programmes or customised tour programmes to suit the preferences of individual tourists, with respect to itinerary, destinations and accommodation and if provision for the transportation of clients is included, such transportation is provided by means of motor vehicles specially hired for the particular purpose by the tour facilitator or provided by a tour and safari operator with whom arrangements have been made by the facilitator for transportation of the clients (Namibia-1on1, n.d.).
6. A sensitisation campaign is primarily meant to create awareness, educate and inform the general public on certain issues.
7. Montessori education is an educational approach characterized by an emphasis on independence, freedom within limits and respect for a child's natural psychological, physical and social development.
8. Site grading is the process of adjusting the slope and elevation of the soil around a home or building.

Table 4.1 **Summary of case organisations and interviewees**

Name of the organisation	Name of the interviewee	Designation of the interviewee	Industry	Type of organisation	Place of operation	Origin of the parent organisation	Brief profile of the organisation	Title of the case study
India Tourism	Madhu Dubey	Regional Director		Government	Australia	India	Nodal agency formulating national policies and programmes for the development and promotion of tourism in India.	India Tourism Sydney: 'Cheerfully Welcoming All to Incredible India!'
Singgasana Hotels and Resorts	Wayan Carma	Director HR and Finance	Tourism and hospitality industry	Local – private	Indonesia	Indonesia	Hospitality management company with deluxe and first-class hotels, residences, a golf course and an international convention center	Singgasana Hotels and Resorts: 'A Majestic Presence with a Promise of Superior Services'
The Grand New Delhi	Deepak Behl	Director HR		Local – private	India	India	One of the reputed 5-star hotels in Delhi	Grand Hotel New Delhi: 'Providing Comfort to Customers'
NA	Eddie Lee	Senior HR professional		MNC	Singapore	Singapore	A major international airways company operating in Singapore	NA

Company								
Officeworks	Martin Duffy	General Manager HR	Retail	Large local	Australia	Australia	Australia's leading retailer and supplier of office products and solutions for home, business and education	Officeworks: 'Taking Care of Big Ideas at Lowest Prices.
Unilever Sri Lanka	Udayan Dutt	Director HR and Corporate Relations		MNC	Sri Lanka	Netherlands and United Kingdom	Giant global fast moving and consumer goods (FMCG) company	Unilever Sri Lanka: 'Winning with People.
Nokia India	NA	NA		MNC	India	Finland	Multinational communications and information technology corporation	Nokia India: 'Connecting People through Innovation and Adapting to Change
GSK China	NA	NA	Healthcare	MNC	China	United Kingdom	Global healthcare company with three primary areas of business — pharmaceuticals, vaccines and consumer healthcare	GSK China: 'Helping People to Do More, Feel Better and Live Longer.
Tata Group	NA	NA	Education	MNC	India	India	Indian conglomerate with over 100 operating companies	Tata Group: 'Bridging Heritage and Innovation in the Education Sector.

(Continued)

Table 4.1 (Continued)

Name of the organisation	Name of the interviewee	Designation of the interviewee	Industry	Type of organisation	Place of operation	Origin of the parent organisation	Brief profile of the organisation	Title of the case study
NA	Rajeev Kumar, ABC	Vice Chair IABC Global Communication Certification Council and General Manager, Learning and Development, Tata Group Corporate Communication		MNC	India	India	NA	NA
AMR India Limited	Manoj Kumar Sharma	Senior Vice President HR	Energy	MNC	India	India	Business conglomerate with businesses in sectors such as mining, constructions, infrastructure and energy	AMR India Limited: 'Growing with Confidence'
JK Organisation	Dilep Misra	President and Head Corporate HR		MNC	India	India	one of India's largest business conglomerates.	JK Organisation: Cementing its century-old 'Caring for People' tradition

References

AIME. (2013). AIME awards celebrate stand excellence and innovation. Paper presented at *Asia-Pacific Incentives and Meetings Expo, Melbourne.* Available from <http://www.aime.com.au/en/Press-Centre/2013-media-releases/AIME-Awards-celebrate-stand-excellence-and-innovation/> Accessed 26.07.13.

AMR. (2013). AMR Group. Available from <http://amrgroup.in/amr_group.html> Accessed 14.03.13.

Arogya World. (2013). *Arogya World and Nokia India engage one million people for mDiabetes through Nokia Life service.* Arogya World. Available from <http://www. arogyaworld.org/arogya-world-and-nokia-india-engage-one-million-people-for-mdiabetes-through-nokia-life-service/> Accessed 06.04.13.

BBC. (2012). Samsung overtakes Nokia in mobile phone shipments. BBC, 27 April 2012. Available from <http://www.bbc.co.uk/news/business-17865117> Accessed 07.04.13.

Bhide, P. V. (2011). JK Group: A coaching style of leadership. *PeopleMatters,* 1 November 2011. Available from <http://www.peoplematters.in/article/2011/11/01/leadership/a-coaching-style-of-leadership/1239> Accessed 10.11.13.

Brand Finance. (2013). *Global 500 2013.* Brand Finance UK. Available from <http://brandirectory.com/league_tables/table/global-500-2013> Accessed 10.07.13.

Business Times. (2013). Unilever Sri Lanka, SLIM launches 'Professional Selling' diploma course. *Business Times,* 27 January 2013. Available from <http://www.sundaytimes.lk/130127/business-times/unilever-sri-lanka-slim-launches-professional-selling-diploma-course-29635.html> Accessed 12.03.13.

BusinessMapsofIndia.com. (n.d.). Nokia India. *Compare Infobase.* Available from <http://business.mapsofindia.com/communications-industry/equipment/nokia.html> Accessed 10.04.13.

Christensen, C. M. (1997). *The innovator's dilemma: When new technologies cause great firms to fail.* Boston, MA: Harvard Business School Press.

CyberMedia. (2013). *Nokia and New India Assurance launch handset insurance plan.* CyberMedia, 13 March 2013. Available from <http://www.ciol.com/ciol/news/185169/nokia-new-india-assurance-launch-handset-insurance-plan> Accessed 10.04.13.

Daily Mirror. (2012). Unilever Sri Lanka wins Gold at HRM Awards 2012. *Daily Mirror,* 10 August 2012. Available from <http://www.dailymirror.lk/business/other/21010-unilever-sri-lanka-wins-gold-at-hrm-awards-2012.html> Accessed 14.03.13.

DailyFT. (2012). Unilever Sri Lanka felicitates Saubhagya star performers. *DailyFT* (Wijeya Newspapers, Sri Lanka). 28 June 2012. Available from <http://www.ft.lk/?s = %22Unilever + Sri + Lanka + felicitates + Saubhagya + star + performers%22> Accessed 10.03.13.

Dutt, U. (2013). Reward demystified. Paper presented at the *Unilever Sri Lanka Annual Meeting at Hilton Colombo Residences, Sri Lanka, 8 April 2013.*

Fernando, M. (2007). Corporate social responsibility in the wake of the Asian tsunami: A comparative case study of two Sri Lankan companies. *European Management Journal,* 25(1), 1–10.

GSK. (2012). *Annual Report 2012.* GlaxoSmithKline. Available from <http://www.gsk.com/content/dam/gsk/globals/documents/pdf/Annual%20Report%202012%20interactive%20version.pdf> Accessed 14.08.13.

GSK. (2013a). *Key achievements.* GlaxoSmithKline. Available from <http://www.gsk.com/about-us/key-achievements.html> Accessed 14.08.13.

GSK. (2013b). *Explore GSK*. GlaxoSmithKline. Available from <http://www.gsk.com/explore-gsk.html> Accessed 14.08.13.

GSK-China. (2013). GSK-China. GlaxoSmithKline-China. Available from <http://www.gsk-china.com/chinese/html/aboutus/gsk-china.html> Accessed 14.08.13.

Hamara Photos. (2010). Sunil Shetty at a charity event held successfully in Chandigarh. Hamara Photos, 24 February 2010. Available from <http://hamaraphotos.com/bollywood/events-and-parties/sunil-shetty-at-a-charity-event-held-successfully-in-chandigarh.html> Accessed 07.03.13.

HBS. (2010). *Harvard Business School receives $50 million gift from the Tata trusts and companies*. Boston, MA: Harvard Business School. Available from <http://www.hbs.edu/news/releases/Pages/tatagift.aspx> Accessed 04.07.13.

Hindustan Times. (2012). JK Paper: A humane work place. Hindustan Times, 22 August 2012. Available from <http://info.shine.com/article/jk-paper-a-humane-work-place/251.html> Accessed 09.11.13.

ICMR. (2006). *The 'Incredible India' campaign: Marketing India to the world*. India: IBS Centre for Management Research. Available from <http://www.icmrindia.org/casestudies/catalogue/Marketing/The%20'Incredible%20India'%20Campaign.htm#Introduction> Accessed 01.02.13.

JKO. (2012). *About JK Organisation*. JK Organisation. Available from <http://jkbschool.org/about-jk-organisation.html> Accessed 20.10.13.

Ladage, R. (2013). Nokia most trusted brand in India. *India Times,* 21 February 2013. Available from <http://www.indiatimes.com/technology/mobile/nokia-most-trusted-brand-in-india-62036.html> Accessed 10.04.13.

Langreth, R. (2011). Andrew Witty's plan to save Glaxo. *Forbes*, 1 July 2011. Available from <http://www.forbes.com/sites/robertlangreth/2011/01/07/andrew-wittys-plan-to-save-glaxo/2/> Accessed 14.08.13.

Manghat, S. (2011). Tata Group identifies three new sectors to drive growth. CNBC-TV18, 30 December 2011. Available from <http://www.moneycontrol.com/news/cnbc-tv18-comments/tata-group-identifies-3-new-sectors-to-drive-growth_641638.html> Accessed 10.07.13.

Martin, P. (2012). Holiday sights shift to China, India. *The Age*, 6 April 2012. Available from <http://www.theage.com.au/travel/travel-news/holiday-sights-shift-to-china-india-20120405-1wfn6.html#ixzz2WovZYzhe>.

Menon, S. (2011). *Training for tomorrow*. Tata Sons. Available from <http://www.tata.com/ourcommitment/articles/inside.aspx?artid = ax%2BTnBkcwJA> Accessed 07.07.13.

MoT. (2012a). *Results − framework document for Ministry of Tourism (2012−2013)*. Ministry of Tourism, Government of India. Available from <http://tourism.gov.in/writereaddata/Uploaded/RFD/050220121004071.pdf> Accessed 10.01.13.

MoT. (2012b). *Hunar-Se-Rozgar Tak − Sena Ke Sahyog Se*. Ministry of Tourism, Government of India. Available from <http://tourism.gov.in/writereaddata/CMSPagePicture/file/Primary%20Content/HRD/rozgarsena.pdf> Accessed 04.04.13.

MoT. (2013a). *Annual Report 2012−2013*. Ministry of Tourism, Government of India. Available from <http://tourism.gov.in/writereaddata/Uploaded/Tender/052420131238134.pdf> Accessed 14.06.13.

MoT. (2013b). *National Tourism Awards 2011−2012*. Ministry of Tourism, Government of India. Available from <http://tourism.gov.in/writereaddata/CMSPagePicture/file/Primary%20Content/Awards/tourism%202011-12%20new.pdf> Accessed 04.04.13.

MoT. (n.d.). *Strategic Action Plan*. Ministry of Tourism, Government of India. Available from <http://tourism.gov.in/writereaddata/Uploaded/ImpDoc/030620120408450.pdf> Accessed 10.01.13.

Mukherjee Saha, J., & Rowley, C. (2013). Karma matters: Business sustainability is beyond just lasting! *World Financial Review, May/June*, 35−38 Available from <http://www.worldfinancialreview.com/?p = 3116> Accessed 04.07.13.

Namibia-1on1. (n.d.). Namibia Tour Facilitators. *Namibia-1on1*. Available from <http://www.namibia-tour-guide.com/namibia-tour-facilitators.html> Accessed 12.10.14.

Nokia. (2012a). *Nokia Sustainability Report 2011*. Nokia. Available from www.nokia.com/sustainability-report Accessed 10.04.13.

Nokia. (2012b). *About Nokia education delivery*. Nokia. Available from <https://projects.developer.nokia.com/NED/wiki> Accessed 15.04.13.

Nokia. (2013). *Nokia Corporation Q4 and full year 2012 Interim Report*. Nokia. Available from <http://www.results.nokia.com/results/Nokia_results2012Q4e.pdf> Accessed 10.04.13.

Officeworks. (2012). *About Us*. Officeworks Australia. Available from <http://www.officeworks.com.au/information/about-us> Accessed 19.11.12.

PIB. (2012). *MoU on campaign Clean India signed between the Ministries of Tourism and Railways*. Press Information Bureau. Available from <http://pib.nic.in/newsite/erelease.aspx?relid = 85228> Accessed 04.04.13.

PIB. (2013). *National tourism awards announced*. Press Information Bureau. Available from <http://www.pib.nic.in/newsite/erelease.aspx?relid = 93499> Accessed 24.04.13.

Questia. (2010). Officeworks notes the numbers with literacy. *The Daily Mercury* (Mackay, Australia), Nokia Corporation Q4 and full year 2012 Interim Report, 2010. Available from <http://www.questia.com/newspaper/1G1-244626103/officeworks-notes-the-numbers-with-literacy> Accessed 09.11.13.

Raman, K., & Ganguli, K. (2010). Education: The next big opportunity. *Tata Review, January*, 67−68.

Rao, N. (2013). Change is the chime. *Tata Review, April*, 45−47.

Shreshtha, A. (2011). *Tata enters education vertical with ClassEdge*. Tata Sons. Available from <http://www.tataclassedge.com/html/aboutus.html> Accessed 07.07.13.

Singgasana Hotels and Resorts. (2013). *About us*. Singgasana Hotels and Resorts. Available from <http://www.singgasanahotels.com/site/hotel> Accessed 24.10.13.

Smedley, T. (2013). Tata's management training director: Sustainability a business necessity. *Guardian Professional*, 9 April 2013. Available from <http://www.guardian.co.uk/sustainable-business/tata-management-director-sustainability-business-necessity> Accessed 04.05.13.

Star News Group. (2012). Tower of green power. *Star Community*, 13 December 2012. Available from <http://dandenong.starcommunity.com.au/journal/2012-12-13/tower-of-green-power-2/> Accessed 12.01.13.

Talreja, V. (2013). Star speakers check in as carrots during downturn *New Indian Express*. Available from <http://newindianexpress.com/business/news/Star-speakers-check-in-as-carrots-during-downturn/2013/08/04/article1716704.ece> Accessed 04.08.13.

Tata Chemicals. (2012). *Swach*. Tata Chemicals. Available from <http://www.tataswach.com/know_tata_swach/smart_choice_of_safety.html> Accessed 10.03.13.

Tata Sons. (2013a). *Tata fast facts*. Tata Sons. Available from <http://www.tata.com/pdf/Tata_fastfacts_final.pdf> Accessed 10.07.13.

Tata Sons. (2013b). *Tatas in education: A fillip for learning.* Tata Sons. Available from <http://www.tata.com/ourcommitment/articles/inside.aspx?artid = yo5Nl5nNlIo> Accessed 01.07.13.

The Australian. (2011). Officeworks defies the gloom. *The Australian,* 11 August 2012. Available from <http://www.theaustralian.com.au/business/companies/officeworks-defies-the-gloom/story-fn91v9q3-1226447908380?nk = a1c8f3faf6a9b1eec5df576960 cd6eea> Accessed 12.01.13.

The Grand. (2013). At a glance. *The Grand New Delhi.* Available from <http://www.the grandnewdelhi.com/> Accessed 01.02.13.

The Island. (2012). Unilever, Ministry of Health to improve hygienic practices in Sri Lanka. The Island, 18 October 2012. Available from <http://www.island.lk/index.php?page_ cat = article-details&page = article-details&code_title = 64053> Accessed 08.03.13.

The Telegraph. (2013). GSK chief Sir Andrew Witty admits compliance failings in China. *The Telegraph,* 24 July 2013. Available from <http://www.telegraph.co.uk/finance/ newsbysector/pharmaceuticalsandchemicals/10199871/GSK-chief-Sir-Andrew-Witty-admits-compliance-failings-in-China.html> Accessed 19.08.13.

TISS. (2013). *About the vocational education programme.* Tata Institute of Social Sciences. Available from <http://sve.tiss.edu/programme> Accessed 04.07.13.

TQMS. (2010). *Innovation.* Tata Quality Management Services. Available from <http:// tqmswebsite.tataquality.com/ui/OtherArticle.aspx?contentid = 091610183151204771> Accessed 10.03.13.

Unilever. (2008). *Introduction to Unilever: February 2008.* London: Unilever.

Unilever. (2012). *Unilever CEO inaugurates new factory in Horana.* Sri Lanka: Unilever. Available from <http://www.unilever.com.lk/aboutus/newsandmedia/pressreleases/ press_releases_2012/PaulPolman_Visit_2012.aspx> Accessed 10.03.13.

Unilever. (2013a). *Unilever sustainable living plan.* Horana, Sri Lanka: Unilever. Available from <http://www.unilever.com.lk/sustainable-living/uslp/> Accessed 10.03.13.

Unilever. (2013b). *Press releases.* Horana, Sri Lanka: Unilever. Available from <http://www. unilever.com.lk/aboutus/newsandmedia/pressreleases/> Accessed 19.03.13.

Unilever. (n.d.). *Our strategy.* Unilever. Available from <http://www.unilever.com/sustain-able-living-2014/our-approach-to-sustainability/our-strategy/> Accessed 10.03.13.

Unilever Careers. (2012). *Udayan Dutt (Director HR, USL) on diversity and inclusion at Unilever.* Horana, Sri Lanka: Unilever. Available from <https://www.facebook.com/notes/ unilever-careers/udayan-dutt-director-hr-usl-on-diversity-and-inclusion-at-the-unilever/ 245346645555573> Accessed 10.03.13.

Wadia, J. (2011). *Excellence in education.* Tata Sons. Available from <http://www.tata.com/ article.aspx?artid = jB/S%2BRa8Bxs = #sthash.zbibQfZl.dpuf> Accessed 07.07.13.

Wang, H. (2012). GSK to develop traditional Chinese medicine. *China Daily,* 7 September 2012. Available from <http://www.chinadaily.com.cn/bizchina/2012-09/07/content_15743913. htm> Accessed 14.08.13.

Wikipedia. (2013). *Atithi Devo Bhav.* Available from <http://en.wikipedia.org/wiki/ Atithi_Devo_Bhav> Accessed 01.02.13.

Worldwatch Institute. (2013). *Crafting a carbon market from India's grassroots.* Washington, DC: Worldwatch Institute.

WTTC. (2012). *India: How does travel & tourism compare to other sectors?* London: World Travel & Tourism Council.

The role of human resources in sustaining the growth of industries

5

Introduction

Human resources has often been regarded as an appendage to an organisation – though, today, the profession has reached a stage where its significance cannot be neglected. Such differences have been operationalised in several theoretical models and frameworks. We will mention just a few here. Tyson and Fell (1986) used an HR model they likened to roles played out on a construction site. They broke it down into three categories, based on criteria such as discretion, planning horizons and roles. The first category was dubbed 'Clerk of Works', a relatively junior role with short-term planning horizons, primarily involved in routine and administrative support, servicing junior line managers, following routines with little discretion and looking for leadership from others. The second category was dubbed 'Contracts Manager', a middle-managerial role with medium-term planning horizons providing knowledge of systems and practices, servicing middle-level line managers with some discretion albeit limited, following and to some extent modifying systems and providing leadership within existing structures. The third category was dubbed 'Architect', acting as a consultant to senior management with long-term planning horizons, conceptualising ideas, solving problems, changing routines and systems, while leading and participating with a great deal of discretion.

An international and leading developer of HR models is Dave Ulrich. Ulrich (1997) broke his HR model down into four roles each based on two dimensions such as operational–strategic and people–process. First, the 'Administrative Expert' develops and executes efficient processes like staffing, training and remuneration. Second, the 'Employee Champion' looks at things from a welfare perspective and attends to employee needs and wishes. Third, the 'Change Agent' initiates and manages change. Fourth, the 'Strategic Partner' looks at both HR and business strategy. Later, Ulrich (2012) developed a framework with six roles. First, the 'Credible Activist' builds personal trust through business acumen. Second, the 'Capability Builder' melds individual abilities into an effective and strong organisation by helping to define and build organisation capabilities. Third, the 'Technology Proponent' accesses, advocates, analyses and aligns technology for the purposes of gathering information, improving efficiency and enhancing relationships. Fourth, the 'Change Champion' connects isolated and independent organisational actions in an effort to integrate and sustain capacity through disciplined change processes. Fifth, the 'HR Innovator and Integrator' innovates and integrates HR practices into unified solutions to solve future business problems. Sixth, the 'Strategic Positioner' thinks and acts from the outside in, is knowledgeable about external business trends and able to translate them into internal decisions and actions.

Welch and Welch (2012) made another interesting contribution to the roles played by HR professionals. They identified the five roles played by HR managers of international projects as 'Service Provider', 'Policy Police', 'Strategic Partner', 'Change Agent' and 'Welfare Officer'. Importantly, they question the simple polar dichotomy of strategic–operational and add another dimension they dub 'Emotional'. They further point out that HR roles are context specific.

The road ahead for HR managers is challenging. There is certainly a need to look again at the abilities of HR professionals to make sure they are well equipped not just for the present but for the future. Chapters 1–4 of this book have clearly demonstrated that many of the challenges faced by HR professionals are similar across industries but that each industry has its own share of specific challenges. Moreover, though globalisation levels things out to a certain degree, each country has its own unique set of characteristics. Some challenges facing the greater Asia Pacific (GAPAC) region differ from those facing the rest of the world. Therefore, knowledge of business dynamisms in specific regions with respect to the rest of the world is essential for the HR professional to be more of a business partner and for businesses to thrive.

If HR professionals believe they can be game changers and have greater strategic and boardroom input, they will need to equip themselves with the new skills and competencies required. Of course, some business managers come up with spurious reasons for not giving HR professionals the respect or importance they deserve. They term HR management as being 'vague', as 'lacking in numbers', as 'having little impact' and so on. In the wake of the 2008 global financial crisis such naive stances do not merit a response. In the following sections we list the key HR challenges facing each of our focus industries and outline possible ways of dealing with them.

How are our focus industries faring in the face of key HR challenges?

In this section we give a quick overview of the core characteristics of our focus industries and the key HR challenges facing them.

Tourism and hospitality

Chapters 1–4 show that the tourism and hospitality industry across the region is growing at a rapid pace, not only adding consistently to national GDP but being a major source of employment too. The demand for tourism products is both domestically driven, as a result of an increase in the number of the middle class and in disposable incomes across the region, and export driven. According to a recent estimate (Advance Tourism, 2010), small and unorganized players dominate the industry. Tourism is a highly competitive resource-intensive industry. Innovative products and services are constantly needed to attract consumers who already have many product choices. Better infrastructure, ensuring the safety and security of visitors, the provision of memorable experiences and efficiency in dealing with emergencies like natural disasters, domestic political uncertainty, economic downturns, terrorism and health pandemics are key to survival of the industry. HR challenges include an acute shortage of skilled HR professionals, talent attraction and engagement, rising cost of labour, diminishing labour productivity, promoting ecofriendly practices, emergency planning for recurrent events like natural disasters and pandemics and safety and security issues.

Retail

The economic growth of a country usually drives growth in the retail industry. Although the retail industry ranges from small family-owned shops and wet markets to global retailers, the norm today includes supermarkets, online shopping carts, social media campaigns, discount labels and multiple offers. The industry is making ever new efforts to entice new customers while meeting its business targets. Employees have one of the lowest workplace engagement index scores of all industries (Kenexa, 2013). The reasons for this include competition being high, the work demanding, having to deal with diverse groups of customers, low pay and poor benefits. HR challenges include talent retention and engagement, training and development, diversity and inclusiveness, workplace safety and security.

Healthcare

Changing demography, fast-ageing populations, longer life expectancy, increases in disposable income, affordability of healthcare services, growing synergy between traditional and modern healthcare practices and the development of newer more innovative products have resulted in the healthcare industry growing at a rapid pace. However, the gap between demand for quality services and the supply of skilled HR is widening. Today, the industry faces an acute shortage of people with the skills the industry needs. The industry needs a major investment in building knowledge, innovative products and the development of intellectual property, areas in which HR professionals have pivotal roles.

Security

Security is a basic human need. The demand for security services has grown enormously in light of security challenges increasing both regionally and globally. Loosely defined, the security industry employs almost twice as many private security personnel than does the government. HR processes in the private and unorganised sector have yet to be formalised. HR challenges include poor incentives, lack of proper training, low employee engagement and selection and inadequate means of screening personnel.

Education

The role played by education in the economic development of a country goes without saying. Education is responsible for the basic skills and HR development of all industries. Yet, the legendary gap between what industry demands and what it gets from academia needs to be bridged. There is an urgent need both for industry-specific curricula that cater for business requirements and for the alignment of education with human capital development. Despite rapidly growing, education has much work to do to attract and retain talent. At the same time, teaching standards need to be improved, a culture of innovation needs to be promoted and the skills of employees regularly updated by providing adequate training and development.

Energy

Like education, the importance of this industry goes without saying for every economic activity needs energy. The exploration, refining and supply of energy to consumers involves many challenges, difficult working conditions and predominantly takes place in remote locations. Despite pay and perks in the industry being higher than in many other industries, this male-dominated industry has an acute shortage of HR professionals with the necessary skills. The industry is known to adopt competitive recruiting strategies, which include taking employees from other organisations and industries and reskilling them. Hence, training and development play vital roles in sustaining business growth. Areas in need of constant attention include workplace safety, environmental protection and innovation.

Summary

The key HR challenges facing these industries are summarised in Tables 5.1 and 5.2. Note that some are common across sectors. Table 5.2 views key HR challenges by occurrence across industries.

Can HR be a game changer in sustaining industry growth?

We summarized our view of the key HR challenges in the previous section. An acute shortage of skilled HR professionals as well as talent attraction and retention have been identified in most of our focus countries as key HR challenges. Yet, how acute is the skills shortage given that globally there are an estimated 205 million unemployed and youth unemployment in some parts of the region is a major concern? Is the term 'skills shortage' a mere fashion statement in the corporate world? Who are the gatekeepers responsible for providing employment opportunities and

Table 5.1 **Summary of key HR challenges identified**

Industry	Growth momentum	Key HR challenges identified
Tourism and hospitality	Rapid	Acute shortage of skilled HR Talent attraction and engagement Rising cost of labour Labour productivity Promoting ecofriendly practices HR planning for emergencies Safety and security issues of visitors
Retail	Based on economic growth of the respective country	Talent retention and engagement Training and development Diversity and inclusiveness Workplace safety and security issues
Healthcare	Rapid	Acute shortage of skilled HR Talent attraction and retention Encouraging innovative culture
Security	Rapid	Employee selection and screening Training and development Employee engagement Poor incentives
Education	Rapid	Talent attraction and retention Performance management Employee engagement Training and development Encouraging innovative culture
Energy	Rapid	Acute shortage of skilled HR Talent attraction and retention Training and development Workplace safety Diversity and inclusiveness Promoting ecofriendly practices Encouraging innovative culture

Table 5.2 Prominent HR challenges across industries

HR challenge	Industry					
	Tourism and hospitality	Retail	Healthcare	Security	Education	Energy
Skilled HR shortages	√	—	√	—	√	√
Talent attraction and retention	√	√	√	—	√	√
Labour costs	√	—	—	—	—	—
Labour productivity	√	√	—	—	—	√
Ecofriendly practices	√	—	—	—	—	√
HR planning for emergencies	√	√	—	—	—	—
Safety and security	—	√	—	√	—	√
Training and development	—	√	—	√	√	√
Diversity and inclusiveness	—	—	—	—	—	√
Innovative cultures	—	—	√	—	√	—
Employee selection	√	√	—	√	—	—
Employee engagement	√	√	—	√	√	—
Incentives	—	—	—	√	—	—
Performance management	—	—	—	—	√	—

√ = prominent across the region; — = does not necessarily mean such challenges are absent.

filling positions in organisations? Are they equipped to decide? Just maybe there are no skills shortages. Could training, mindset change and reskilling solve the possible 'mirage' of skill shortages?

Krugman (2014) believes there is no skills gap and that the term is a zombie idea.[1] He notes that today's researchers have time and again confirmed that the skills gap is little more than an overreaction on the part of employers who seem to find it fashionable to keep the topic alive. In a similar vein, Cappelli (2012) notes that many organisations complicate the hiring process by expecting too much from candidates. In pursuit of getting the right fit for the role, organisations are known to have added so many job requirements as to make the position almost surreal. For instance, Cappelli (2012) quoted a position that had gone unfilled for nearly a year where the employer was expecting the candidate not only to be the HR expert but also the marketing, publishing, project manager, accounting and finance expert as well. Cappelli (2012) believes such perceptions of a skills shortage are actually self-inflicted rather than a real challenge. Organisations often prefer to hire ready-made employees who require no training rather than training or reskilling candidates to make them suitable for the position.

Many researchers have identified talent management as a top priority for organisations. Attracting, developing, managing performance, retaining talent, keeping HR engaged while removing underperformers are essential elements of talent management (Lockwood, 2006). Talent management has to deal with uncertainty and rapidly changing business dynamism.[2] In such a scenario, there are inherent risks facing talent management and the way in which they are managed is of utmost importance. Cappelli (2008) points out that such risks include the costs of a mismatch between employees and skills and the costs of losing investments in talent by failing to retain employees. So, what can the HR professional do to make talent management effective? Ulrich, Younger, Brockbank, and Ulrich (2012) note that good HR talent management starts with the end in mind.

The HR professional can create value by improving the performance and flexibility of talent and in this way help develop organisation capability. The HR professional must be equipped with the requisite skills and competencies for this to be achieved. A talent strategy that is properly formulated can avoid many organisational tragedies, but the converse is true (Mukherjee Saha, 2012). When formulating a talent management strategy care must be taken to keep diversity and inclusiveness in mind (diversity includes such things as gender, age, ethnicity, culture, ability, education and religion).

HR selection and screening was recently identified as a key threat to corporate America. Research shows that résumé fraud, which includes the fabrication of degrees and the falsification of credentials, occurs at every level in every type of organisation – be it the most elite academic institution or corporate sector of repute. According to a 2002 study by the Association of Certified Fraud Examiners (ACFE) such frauds cost corporate America US$600 billion annually (Walker, Glovka, Greenawalt, & McNulty, 2013).

HR planning needs to be competency based for it to assist in the planning, prevention, protection, response and recovery after an emergency like a natural disaster, pandemic or terrorist attack. Competency is defined as a combination of the knowledge, skills, ability and judgement required to perform safely and ethically in a designated role or setting. Such activities could involve the collection of quantitative data (such as providers available, demographics and attack rates) and qualitative data (collected from focus groups and stakeholder discussions on related matters like the productivity of healthcare providers and staff allocation challenges). Such HR planning should also consider the ability and willingness of employees to work at times of emergency when loyalty to the job may conflict with concern about families. For instance, one study of emergency services personnel predicted that in the event of an influenza pandemic only 49 per cent would continue to work and the rest would prefer to stay at home (MoH, 2012, p. 12; Walker et al., 2013).

Chapters 1−4 have shown that, despite the region being one of the most disaster-prone zones of the world, few countries and organisations have institutionalised ecofriendly practices. There are conflicting views as to whether the promotion of ecofriendly practices should be the responsibility of HRM and, if so, what role HRM could play in influencing an organisation's sustainability agenda. HRM could take a leading role in an organisation's sustainability agenda but, first, it needs to have a good understanding of what sustainability is all about, what it means for the organisation and the business impact of adhering to ecofriendly practices.

Research suggests there is a connection between strategic HRM and firm innovation. Afuah (1998) believes innovation to be of two types: (1) product innovation in which new products or services are introduced to meet an external or market need; (2) process innovations in which new production or service operations are introduced within the organisation. HRM can play a significant role in process innovation by acquiring and matching the right skills for the right roles at the right times. It could also help in recording industry best practices and communicating them within organisations. It could further develop cultural and social norms as a means of executing strategies. HRM can use a number of levers, like performance management, rewards and recognition, talent management, organisational design and internal communication, to convey and set innovation expectations and reinforce good practices by rewards and recognition. HRM can help in identifying critical roles and effectively manage talent. It can also help in designing organisational structures, processes, roles, capabilities, etc. to meet innovation objectives while effectively communicating and reinforcing the culture of innovation (KPMG, 2013; Siengthai & Bechter, 2001).

HRM plays a significant role in health and safety, protection of assets and the environment. For instance, when Chevron Singapore successfully introduced a number of unique health, environment and safety (HES) strategies, this positively impacted its employee engagement scores. Singapore is the regional headquarters of Chevron's downstream[3] operations in the region, which include the company's manufacturing, supply and trading, marketing and lubricants businesses. In Singapore the company spends over SG$800,000 on health benefits and promotions annually. Apart from workplace safety training for its employees, free flu vaccinations and complimentary health screening, all employees are issued with ergonomic furniture such as sit-to-stand tables and ergonomic chairs. Sit-to-stand tables were selected to promote the posture of staff who alternate between sitting and standing throughout the working day. All Chevron computers are installed with WorkPace break software. The software tracks the frequency and degree of an employee's computer usage and prompts employees to take stretch breaks and micro pauses at intervals. It suggests the best times for taking breaks and gives prompts via an on-screen warning when the recommended typing speed or usage time has been exceeded. WorkPace also provides on-screen exercises and stretches for employees to follow in an effort to prevent repetitive stress injury. The company's HES efforts have helped reduce employee absenteeism and improved employee productivity, thereby contributing to the economic bottom line of the organisation (Chevron, 2008).

Without exception, the HR/business leaders we interviewed believed that HR plays a major role in sustaining industries. Burdened with so many responsibilities though, there is a concern that HR professionals are overworked. Is there anything out there that can be used to assist them?

PROACT to sustain

Recent records show that globally there are close to one million HR professionals catering for 3 billion employed and determining the fate of 205 million unemployed in one way or another. This is far below the benchmark HR-to-employee ratio of 1:100. Against a backdrop of fast-growing industries, demand for quality products and services and increasing demand for improvements in labour productivity, how can HR become a game changer and leverage the people power needed for sustainability (Evans, 2011; Russell & Harrop, 2005; Woods, 2012)?

Game changers are people who transform the accepted rules, processes, strategies and management of business functions. Has HR as a profession progressed and changed enough to play a leading role in sustaining businesses? Can HR actively participate in both regular maintenance and at the same time withstand contingencies? We think there is much more to be done. As a Society for Human Resource Management report notes, there is a widening gap between the capabilities of those working in HR and the business acumen needed for them to be successful strategic partners in a business organisation (SHRM, 2005). There are many uncertainties in the business environment and those professionals who understand the principles of uncertainty and react to the changing environment often survive better than the rest. By reducing uncertainties HR may play a key role in sustaining businesses. By adhering to the PROACT (Perceive and Recognise, Observe, Alert, consider Contingencies and Team up to act) framework, HR could attain the status of game changer and help sustain businesses and organisations (Mukherjee Saha & Ang, 2012) (Table 5.3).

Table 5.3 PROACT framework

Parameters	Brief description
Perceive and Recognise (PR)	Perceive and recognise the need to skill up and upgrade on a regular basis to cope with the changing business environment
Observe (O)	Observe the actions of relevant stakeholders and engage with them on a regular basis to get a feel for ground realities
Alert (A)	Alert senior management and regularly appraise them of changing scenarios
Consider Contingencies (C)	Assess and consider contingencies that may affect the functioning of the business and people systems
Team up to act (T)	Team up with relevant stakeholders to act and take the necessary remedial measures

Conclusion

This chapter briefly discusses the way in which HR has changed over the years and summarises the key HR challenges facing our focus industries across the GAPAC region. It also raises a few questions on issues like skills shortages, talent attraction and retention. Of the many ways HR could help sustain business growth, we believe HR could become a game changer by adopting the PROACT framework. Finally, we move on to our concluding chapter in the hope that our 'thoughts will become things'!

Notes

1. Krugman defines a zombie idea as 'a proposition that has been thoroughly refuted by analysis and evidence, and should be dead — but won't stay dead because it serves a political purpose, appeals to prejudices, or both.'
2. Business dynamism is a process in which businesses are continually born, fail, expand and contract as a result of jobs being created, destroyed or turned over.
3. Downstream refers to the refining of crude oil and the processing and purifying of natural gas.

References

Advance Tourism. (2010). Tourism is an industry of small businesses. *Advance Tourism*. Available from: <http://www.advancetourism.com.au/files/NGGO2Q9JW7/JG_1_Tourism_is_about_small_businesses.pdf> Accessed 14.01.14.

Afuah, A. (1998). *Innovation management: Strategies, implementation*. Oxford, UK: Oxford University Press.

Cappelli, P. (2008). *The talent on demand approach*. Harvard Business Publishing. Available from: <http://www.talentondemand.org/toda.pdf>.

Cappelli, P. (2012). The skills gap myth: Why companies can't find good people. *business.time.com*, 4 June 2012. Available from: <http://business.time.com/2012/06/04/the-skills-gap-myth-why-companies-cant-find-good-people/>.

Chevron. (2008). Chevron − HR practices. Paper presented to the Panel of Judges for evaluation for The Singapore HR Awards 2009, *SHRI, Singapore, 9 April 2008*.

Evans, L. (2011). Global employment: What is the world employment rate? *The Guardian*, 25 January 2011. Available from: <http://www.theguardian.com/news/datablog/2011/jan/25/global-economy-globalrecession>.

Kenexa. (2013). *The world of retail: How employee engagement can help the registers ring.* Wayne, PA: Kenexa.

KPMG. (2013). *HR as a driver for organizational innovation*. North Holland, the Netherlands: KPMG.

Krugman, P. (2014). Jobs and skills and zombies. *New York Times*, 31 March, 2014. Available from: <http://www.nytimes.com/2014/03/31/opinion/krugman-jobs-and-skills-and-zombies.html> Accessed 5.04.14.

Lockwood, N. R. (2006). *Talent management: Driver for organizational success*. SHRM Research Quarterly, 2, 2−10. Available from: <http://www.shrm.org/research/articles/articles/documents/0606rquartpdf.pdf> Accessed 05.04.14

MoH. (2012). *British Columbia's Pandemic Influenza Response Plan (2012): Human resource planning guideline*. Victoria, BC: Ministry of Health, Province of British Columbia.

Mukherjee Saha, J. (2012). *Talent strategies to avoid talent tragedies*. HR Matters (Malaysia). April.

Mukherjee Saha, J., & Ang, D. (2012). *Being a game changer: Role of HR in business sustainability*. Arabian Society for Human Resource Management (Abu Dhabi). March 25−8.

Russell, R., & Harrop, D. (2005). Staffing the human resources function. Available from: <www.rsmmcgladrey.com >.

SHRM. (2005). *Why we hate HR?* Alexandria, VA: Society for Human Resource Management.

Siengthai, S., & Bechter, C. (2001). Strategic human resource management and firm innovation. *Research and Practice in Human Resource Management, 9*(1), 35−57.

Tyson, S., & Fell, A. (1986). *Evaluating the personnel function*. London: Hutchinson.

Ulrich, D. (1997). *Human resource champions: The next agenda for adding value and delivering results*. Cambridge, MA: Harvard Business School Press.

Ulrich, D. (2012). *Human resource competency study 2012*. Provo, UT: RBL Group USA.

Ulrich, D., Younger, J., Brockbank, W., & Ulrich, M. (2012). HR talent and the new HR competencies. Provo, UT: RBL Group USA. Available from: <http://rbl-net.s3.amazonaws.com/hrcs/2012/HRtalent-HRcompetencies.pdf> Accessed 23.02.14.

Walker, D., Glovka, L., Greenawalt, B., & McNulty, J. (2013). *Top security threats and management issues facing corporate America*. New York: Securitas Security Services.

Welch, C., & Welch, D. (2012). What do HR managers do? HR roles on international projects. *Management International Review, 52*(4), 597−617.

Woods, D. (2012). The six competencies to inspire HR professionals for 2012. *HR Magazine*, 4 January 2012. Available from: <http://www.hrmagazine.co.uk/hr/features/1020649/exclusive-the-competencies-inspire-hr-professionals-2012#sthash.1UumsnVC.dpuf> interviews by DAVID WOODS, Accessed 14.03.14.

Conclusion

6

Introduction

We wrote this book to investigate how the policies and practices of the HR profession and function have impacted people across the greater Asia Pacific (GAPAC) region. In particular, we were interested in how HR practitioners are dealing with the key HR issues and challenges facing important industries in the region and how this has impacted organisations and performance. We wanted to understand the extent to which human resource management (HRM) had evolved and how the different typologies and frameworks reflected reality (Rowley & Jackson, 2011).

At the time of writing this book, we were interested in the creative power of thought in which thoughts become things. This phenomenon has its basis in the laws of attraction and the art of collective thinking. Science has shown us that every thought has a frequency and that, by concentrating on a single thought, we emit and enable that frequency on a consistent basis. This made us wonder whether every thought originating at the individual level might filter through organisations to industries and broadly to societies at large (Mukherjee Saha, 2010). In a way, our book reinforces such a phenomenon by adopting a distinctive approach to HRM in which HR collaborates with line managers in carrying out people-oriented organisational activities (Rowley & Jackson, 2011). Today's dynamic business environment demands HR's role be more proactive, coherent and connected, while being collaborative with line managers.

Content overview

Chapter 1 introduced the context of the book. It noted the various typologies and frameworks used in HRM. It presented data to support the growing significance of the GAPAC region. The issues, challenges, prospects and unique identities of each of the 17 economies in the region were discussed. Six focus industries – tourism and hospitality, retail, healthcare, security, education and energy – were briefly analysed and the key concomitant HR issues and challenges noted. These industries are key contributors to economies and major sources of employment. The chapter presented the research and methods used to investigate the changing role and significance of HR in the region.

Chapter 2 outlined the country-specific issues and challenges of the six focus industries in each of the 17 economies in the region. The chapter broadly presented key statistics on the industries, which included total contribution to employment such as the number of jobs generated directly in the industry, indirect and induced contributions and total contribution to GDP. The interdependency of the industries was clearly established.

To investigate the changing HR landscape across the region, Chapter 3 used ten parameters of labour market efficiency and compared the global and regional rankings of our 17 focus economies between 2008 and 2013. Emphasis was put on labour markets having the flexibility to shift workers from one economic activity to another rapidly and at low cost and on facilitating wage fluctuations without much social disruption. The importance of the latter has been dramatically highlighted by recent events in Arab countries. It was high youth unemployment in Tunisia that sparked the social unrest that spread across the region. Efficient labour markets must ensure a clear relationship between worker incentives and efforts to promote meritocracy at the workplace. They must also provide equity between women and men in the business environment. The chapter ended by examining the social media profiles of ten senior HR professionals in each of the 17 economies across the region to get a feel for the HR profession in the region.

Chapter 4 consisted of ten case studies from organisations in our focus industries operating in the region. It examined how these organisations dealt with business and HR challenges. The chapter gave answers to the following fundamental questions relating to these organisations:

- What were the key industry-specific HR/business challenges?
- How prepared were HR professionals to deal with such challenges?
- Could HR become a game changer?
- What role could HR play in minimising business risks and sustaining industry growth?

Chapter 5 summarised how HR could be key to creating economic, environmental and social growth. It briefly noted the core characteristics and key HR challenges facing organisations across the region. The chapter listed 14 HR challenges and compared them across the six industries. The PROACT framework was also introduced. Its adoption may well make HR a game changer when it comes to sustaining industries. The chapter went on to advocate that properly aligned HR policies and practices could provide a direct and economically significant contribution to organisational performance.

Discussion

The book has looked at the important and critical economies of the GAPAC region and presented comparative, economic, industrial and HRM details on organisations in six key sectors as well as the challenges facing them. Yet, as Chapters 1–5 have made abundantly clear, countries and organisations in the region vary widely. This has important implications both practically and theoretically. Practically, there are doubts whether the notions of globalisation and so-called 'best practice' (Rowley & Wei, 2011) lead to convergence of HRM or not. Theoretically, there remain doubts about universalism, not only in business systems, but also HR policy and practice (Rowley & Benson, 2002).

The book considered a number of typologies put forward by HR practitioners and how best to implement them. Among the best known were those proposed by Dave Ulrich (Ulrich, 1997; Ulrich, Younger, Brockbank, & Ulrich, 2012). The book extended Ulrich's HR business partner concept to that of 'HR as a player' and advocated that HR professionals must learn to coach, design, build, facilitate, lead and give business leaders a conscience if they want to become players (Ulrich & Beatty, 2001). There are other typologies (Caldwell, 2003; Storey, 1992) that are similar in terms of role categorization and the strategic−operational dichotomy (Welch & Welch, 2012).

Some of the typologies put forward by such HR practitioners as Dave Ulrich have been questioned and criticised on various grounds (Welch & Welch, 2012), including feasibility (Caldwell, 2008; Wood, 1999), oversimplification of complex roles and underemphasis of conflict and role descriptions (Stiles & Trevor, 2006). Nevertheless, it is the very simplicity of a typology that provides analytical usefulness and practical impact. Furthermore, it does not necessarily follow that such works are primarily targeting academics as the ultimate audience. On the contrary, they are targeting HR practitioners themselves who are known to be a much more tricky audience to reach, yet alone influence. Such a target requires a very different style, content and presentation of materials to make an impact, especially one that is lasting.

Conclusion

The book has looked at the HR profession and HR practices across six focus industries in the GAPAC region. The different HR typologies and models show that the work done by HR managers is wide ranging, with the responsibilities of an HR manager in one organization being totally different from those of an HR manager in another organisation. The purpose of the book is to help progress the HR profession by listing the key challenges it faces, identifying the necessary skills and competencies required of a HR manager, while gathering evidence to reinforce our conviction that HR can be a game changer in sustaining industries. Finally, despite Western typologies of HRM having analytical usefulness, it seems a more distinctive 'Asian HRM' (Rowley, Benson, & Warner, 2004) will prevail in the region as a result of institutional and cultural underpinning. The book could represent a clarion call for more Asia-centric frameworks and typologies, models and theorizing.

References

Caldwell, R. (2003). The changing roles of personnel managers: Old ambiguities, new uncertainties. *Journal of Management Studies, 40*(40), 983−1004.

Caldwell, R. (2008). HR business partner competency models: Recontextualising HRM. *International Studies of Management and Organisation, 29*(4), 6−23.

Mukherjee Saha, J. (2010). *HR transmutation: Path to progress.* Singapore: Human Capital Singapore, pp. 21−22.

Rowley, C., & Benson, J. (2002). Convergence and divergence in Asian HRM. *California Management Review, 44*(2), 90−109.

Rowley, C., Benson, J., & Warner, M. (2004). Towards an Asian model of HRM: Comparative analysis of China, Japan and Korea. *International Journal of HRM, 15* (4/5), 917−933.

Rowley, C., & Jackson, K. (2011). *Human resource management: The key concepts.* London: Taylor & Francis.

Rowley, C., & Wei, Q. (2011). Best practice. In C. Rowley, & K. Jackson (Eds.), *Human resource management: The key concepts* (pp. 7−10). London: Routledge.

Stiles, P., & Trevor, J. (2006). The human resource department: Roles, coordination and influence. In G. K. Stahl, & I. Björkman (Eds.), *Handbook of research in international human resource management* (pp. 4−67). London: Edward Elgar.

Storey, J. (1992). *Developments in the management of human resources.* Oxford: Blackwell.

Ulrich, D. (1997). *Human resource champions.* Boston, MA: Harvard Business School Press.

Ulrich, D., & Beatty, D. (2001). From partners to players: Extending the HR playing field. *Human Resource Management, 40*(4), 293−307.

Ulrich, D., Younger, J., Brockbank, W., & Ulrich, M. (2012). *HR talent and the new HR competencies.* Provo, UT: RBL Group. (RBL White Paper Series).

Welch, C., & Welch, D. (2012). What do HR managers do? HR roles on international projects. *Management International Review, 52*(4), 597−617.

Wood, S. (1999). HRM and performance. *International Journal of Management Reviews, 1*(4), 367−413.

Index

Note: Page numbers followed by '*t*' refer to tables.

Printed and bound by CPI Group (UK) Ltd, Croydon, CR0 4YY

08/05/2025

01864968-0001